OLD TOWN HALLS OF CHRISTCHURCH

W. A. HOODLESS

NATULA PUBLICATIONS

This edition published in 2009 by Natula Publications,
Christchurch, Dorset BH23 1JD
On behalf of Christchurch Local History Society

© W.A. Hoodless 2009

The right of W. A. Hoodless B.Sc., M.R.I.C.S. to be identified as the author of this work has been asserted by him in accordance with the Copyright, Designs and Patent Act 1988.

ISBN 9781897887783

A CIP catalogue record of this book is available from the British Library.

All rights reserved. No part of this publication may be reproduced, stored in a retrieval system, or transmitted in any form or by any means (electronic, mechanical, photocopying, recording or otherwise) without the prior permission of the copyright holder.

Printed by Cpod, Trowbridge, Wiltshire.

Front cover picture: The 'Mayor's Parlour' today.
Photographed by the Author.

A recent picture of the remaining part of the last Town Hall referred to in the book. The 'Mayor's Parlour' of today is a most attractive link to the long and distinguished history of local administration in Christchurch.

Back cover picture: An etching in black and white by Benjamin Ferrey from around 1830; subsequently coloured.
(Reproduced by courtesy of the Red House Museum, Christchurch)

A painting from the time of the horse and cart. The quoin stones of the Third Town Hall on the right of the picture were re-used for the 'Mayor's Parlour' shown on the front cover of the book. An early plan had been to enclose the ground floor of the Third Hall and extend it with a covered staircase. That would have been placed on the west end of the south elevation that we can see in the picture, facing Church Street.

CONTENTS

		Page
Frontispiece	Admiral Walcott	v
List of illustrations		vii
Preface		ix
Foreword		xiii
Chapter One	Life and times of the 'Old Tolsey'	1
Chapter Two	Fifteenth century and a new hall	11
Chapter Three	Third Town Hall in mid-street	23
Chapter Four	Resolution: upgrade as existing	35
Chapter Five	U-turn: we must relocate to a big site	41
Chapter Six	Planning the fourth hall	51
Chapter Seven	Fraught but in the end triumphant	57
Chapter Eight	Controversies and comment	65
Chapter Nine	Town Hall gatherings	75
Chapter Ten	From 1860 hall to 1960 demolition plan	83
Chapter Eleven	The 'Mayor's Parlour' today	93
Index		95

CHRISTCHURCH LOCAL HISTORY SOCIETY

The Society is dedicated to the study of the past of our ancient borough and the preservation of all aspects of our surviving heritage. We are unusual in having an archive collection to manage, as well as all the other aspects of a thriving organisation. These include regular talks and events, the publication of a range of books and the issue of a regular Journal.

Currently we have over 350 members and membership is open to anyone with an interest in any aspect of the Local History of Christchurch. To find out more contact us at our History Room in the Christchurch Library, High Street, Christchurch BH23 1AW.

Further information can be found on our website at the following address:-

www.historychristchurch.org

Other Books By the Same Author

Hengistbury Head, The Whole Story (Poole Historical Trust 2005)
Air Raid, A Diary and Stories from the Essex Blitz (History Press 2008)

Admiral John Edward Walcott C.B.E., M.P. (1790-1868)
(Photograph of an 1857 portrait by Lewis Holloway and reproduced with the kind permission of the Russell-Cotes Art Gallery and Museum.)

Admiral Walcott was a generous and popular M.P. for Christchurch and the person responsible in 1855 for persuading the Corporation to build a new Town Hall instead of altering the 1746 one. This portrait was presented to the Inhabitants of Christchurch by his daughter Constance on 4th February 1871 and duly hung in the Town Hall's Council Chamber south of the fireplace.

LIST OF ILLUSTRATIONS

		Page
Fig. 1	Four old Town Halls of Christchurch on 1843 Tithe Map extract	2
Fig. 2	Current Building on the Old Tolsey site, now occupied by The Carphone Warehouse	4
Fig. 3	Building erected on the site of the Old Tolsey, about 100 years after its demolition	7
Fig. 4	Typical Town Hall which may be like the Tolsey (Second Town Hall)	9
Fig. 5	Present-day restoration of Titchfield Town Hall	12
Fig. 6	Dedication of the Old Minute Book	14
Fig. 7	Town Goods of Christchurch	16
Fig. 8	First Mace of the Corporation	18
Fig. 9	Corporation Accounts from November 1703	20
Fig. 10	Third Town Hall at the end of Castle Street	22
Fig. 11	High Street celebration of the Reform Act 1832	24
Fig. 12	Most detailed view existing of the Third Town Hall	26
Fig. 13	Setting of the 1746 Town Hall based on the 1843 Tithe Map	27
Fig. 14	Position of the Third Town Hall marked by five ex-Mayors	30
Fig. 15	Group photograph of the five ex-Mayors	31
Fig. 16	Watercolour of Castle Street c. 1830	33
Fig. 17	The Corporation's attempt to solve the traffic problem in 1834	36
Fig. 18	Rope for the Town Clock	38

LIST OF ILLUSTRATIONS (continued)

		Page
Fig. 19	Upgrade plan dated 1855 for the Third Town Hall	42
Fig. 20	Part of first floor upgrade plan dated 1855	43
Fig. 21	John Edward Holloway (1821-1901)	47
Fig. 22	James Druitt (1816-1904)	48
Fig. 23	View across the High Street c. 1865 after demolition of the Third Town Hall	50
Fig. 24	Fourth Town Hall in 1870	52
Fig. 25	Setting of the Fourth Town Hall in 1974	56
Fig. 26	Edward VII Coronation Parade in Christchurch High Street, August 1902	62
Fig. 27	Christchurch Choral Society concert programme in 1893	74
Fig. 28	The Fourth Town Hall in 1860	82
Fig. 29	Scheme for new Town Hall with 1960 Compulsory Purchase Order	86
Fig. 30	Satirical sketch of alternative scheme from Borough Engineer in 1961	90

PREFACE

Christchurch has coined the expression 'Where Time is Pleasant' and with considerable justification. Although historically a fairly poor town, it has now capitalised well on its idyllic setting between the Rivers Stour and Avon and on a host of heritage features. I am sure that both residents and visitors know they are fortunate to be in such a place. Generally, a heritage feature, which seems at first glance to be simply an old building, turns out to have a lively history and even antecedents. So it is with the current 'Mayor's Parlour' in front of Saxon Square.

Naturally, the further back in time one goes, the harder it is to find out what happened in any particular case. Nonetheless, it has proved possible to piece together some history of the town's place of administration from the early Middle Ages. The very first Town Hall that we know about was itself replaced, probably in the 15th century. Altogether four old Town Halls are covered, excluding the current Civic Offices in Bridge Street. In order to be as clear as possible in this book, they are simply named as the First, Second, Third and Fourth Town Halls. They were located respectively at the corner of High Street and Millhams Street; at the junction of Castle Street, Church Street and High Street; the same again; and finally, at what is now Saxon Square.

Perhaps the most important account of the book concerns the rather traumatic relocation of the 1746 Third Town Hall which really had outlived its usefulness over 100 years later. The culture of Victorian Britain was very different from that of today, as can be seen in the reports and letters included here. A strong sense of duty, and indeed humour, is very evident. At the time of publication, it is around 150 years since that 1860 event, one well worthy of celebration by both Christchurch Borough Council and the Christchurch Local History Society.

In addition to the Town Hall buildings themselves, are matters connected with the people of the town and their experiences. After all, a Town Hall is just a means to an end – its purpose is to organise the affairs of the town within its remit, and to the benefit of those who live there. And so the book goes beyond simply the structures in order to touch upon some issues and events that were connected to the town and its place of administration – in short the work of the Mayor and Burgesses.

When looking at the 'Mayor's Parlour' fronting Saxon Square, it is strange to reflect that it was partly constructed with stones first used in 1746. Even more strange is the surreal picture conjured up by a correspondent to the local newspaper at the time of removal – a bodily relocation on wheels along the High Street! But apart from such humour, there were serious debates on how to resolve the problem of the unsatisfactory existing hall. In one disagreement, the casting vote of a committee chairman was required to decide where to place it on the site. In another case, a subscription argument verged on acrimony with the most detailed justifications on both sides, published for all to see. Yet determination, to see the project through, won the day and there was a fine improvement for the town.

In summary, although a major story of the book is about the relocation project and the very human forces which surrounded it, an attempt has also been made to piece together the life and times of all four old Town Halls. For instance connected matters are mentioned, such as the Town Goods, some decisions of the old Corporation and Town Hall entertainment in Victorian Christchurch.

I feel privileged to be asked to write a book on such a subject and would like to thank the many people who have been so helpful. In no particular order, these are John Lewis from the Red House Museum; Ian Messer, Mike Andrews, Mike Tizzard, Jane Rutter and the helpers in the Local History Room of the Christchurch Local History Society; Ian Stevenson; Sue Newman; David Flagg, the current Mayor of Christchurch; the Russell-Cotes Art Gallery and Museum; Dorchester architect, Anthony Jaggard; Sue Besant, Allan Wood and other staff from Christchurch Borough Council; Jane Martin of Natula Publications; ex-Mayors Ed Coope, Mike Hodges, Mike Winfield, Mrs. Norma Fox and David Fox for being good sports in the 'Town Hall in the road' photograph; Ted Baker for some transcriptions and translations; Mark Forrest and others at the Dorset History Centre; David Eels; and Richard Harris from the Weald and Downland Museum.

Regarding sources, some of the book's material is held at the Dorset History Centre in Dorchester and used with the Centre's permission. Thanks are also due to the Hampshire County Council Museums Service, Red House Museum. Where material is still in copyright, I believe that I have the permission of the owners to reproduce it. I would be glad to be advised if I have unwittingly infringed any person's rights.

Finally, I would mention that 'Mayor's Parlour' has been used throughout the book to denote the remains of the Fourth Town Hall, which still fronts Saxon Square today, as this is the name in common usage for it and also to avoid confusion as this building at 30 High Street is now strictly called the Old Town Hall.

FOREWORD

Christchurch Borough Council and Christchurch Local History Society are very pleased to support the publication of this new book about the Town Halls of Christchurch. It is a fascinating story, which has never been written before, concerning not only the buildings but also the human interest of how decisions were made in earlier years by those in authority.

We must take this opportunity to thank Bill Hoodless, the author, who has put the book together. The research involved has been enormous and amount of information he has unearthed is amazing. Having assembled the facts it is another matter to put them into a readable book and we congratulate him on this achievement.

There are two reasons for producing the book at this time. One is that it is the 150th anniversary of the decision to move the Old Town Hall from the market square at the junction of Church Street, High Street and Castle Street to where it now stands in the High Street; quite an exercise in 1859.

The second reason is to celebrate the 20th anniversary of the founding of the Christchurch Local History Society. Over the years the Society has been involved in the publication of a number of books about the history of Christchurch and we are very happy to have had an opportunity to be associated with this one.

Finally, to you the reader, we hope you enjoy the book and that it gives you an insight into the history of Christchurch and how things were organised in the past.

David Flagg
Mayor
Christchurch Borough Council

Ian Messer
Chairman
Christchurch Local History Society

CHAPTER ONE

LIFE AND TIMES OF THE 'OLD TOLSEY'

It may be best to begin with the word 'Tolsey' (other spellings include Tolsye, Tolsylde and Tolseyle) which has its own meaning in the language: a tollbooth, merchants' meeting place or exchange. The name itself suggests a place where market tolls were collected. Commonly, a Tolsey would include an upper chamber and open ground level for market stalls, particularly those selling goods needing protection from the weather. Such a building allowed officials to oversee the market proceedings from the upper level, so explaining a tendency to prominent positions with views along more than one street. Certainly in Christchurch, the hall described in the next chapter known as simply the 'Tolsey', was so located. In later years, part of or the whole of the ground area was sometimes enclosed. Although the main function was market-related, town meetings could also be held on the first floor, so making these structures an early form of Town Hall.

A market has been held in Christchurch for most of the last millennium and since the Norman Conquest indications are that there has been a regular market from about 1150 or possibly earlier. As recorded on the plaque on the 'Mayor's Parlour', the market closed in 1871 and re-opened in 1976. A trader would expect to pay a toll on the goods he was selling and a charge for being allowed to erect a stall, known as stallage. A market bell could be rung on Market Day to signify the start and end of trading for the day. The open ground level of a Tolsey could be used for storing the stalls whilst any miscreants could face a court held in the chamber upstairs – hence again the prominent siting of such places giving the market officials a good outlook.

The Market Toll House, or Old Tolsey, was the Town Hall, from an uncertain date in the Middle Ages up to probably the 15th century. The word 'probably' has to be used here due to a small element of uncertainty and a need to interpret some historical evidence. For our purposes however, this is deemed to be the first Christchurch Town Hall. Since this chapter has to deal with the time that the Old Tolsey stopped being a Town Hall, there is some discussion below of the leases granted on the next one, the Tolsey. It is these leases which indicate that Christchurch's first Town Hall relocation happened at the end of the 15th century.

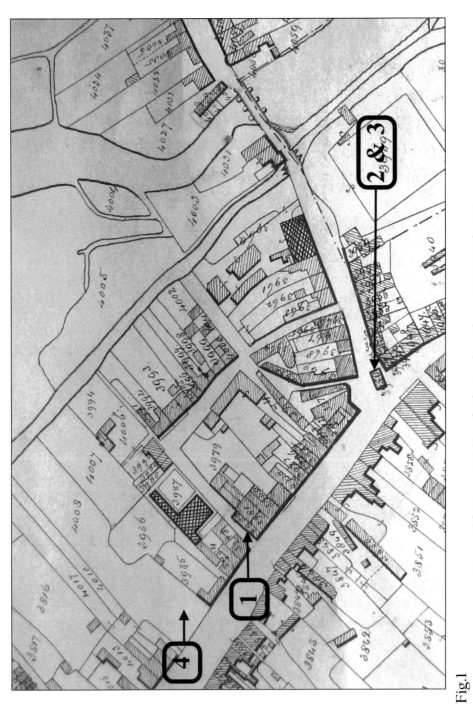

Fig.1

Four old Town Halls of Christchurch on 1843 Tithe Map extract
(Map reproduced by courtesy of the Dorset History Centre Ref. T/CC)

This first illustration may help identification. Numbered sites are in date order:
1. First Town Hall – early Middle Ages to probably 15th Century; 2. Second Town Hall – probably 15th century to c. 1746;
3. Third Town Hall – c.1746 to 1859; 4. Fourth Town Hall – 1860 to present time as 'Mavor's Parlour'.

As long ago as the 14th century, it is believed that the Borough or Corporation of Christchurch had a seal that was used by the Mayor and Burgesses for the purpose of executing legal documents. The seal has been reproduced in a circular window at the current Town Hall, as shown in the photograph at the Foreword to this book. It is above the heads of Ian Messer the present (2009) Chairman of the Christchurch Local History Society and David Flagg the Mayor of the Borough. The Saviour is depicted on a throne within a niche. Whilst His right hand is raised as in an act of benediction, in His left hand are the holy writings. The legend is: 'S: COMVNE: VILLE: XPI: ECCLIE DE TWINHAM' translating as 'The Common Seal of the Town of Christchurch-Twynham'. The seal demonstrates continuity of local administration from the First Town Hall to the latest one built in 1980, a period of around 600 years.

The Old Tolsey site in the High Street adjoins what is now the Ship Inn on one side and Millhams Street on the other. To avoid confusion, *Fig.1* is an 1843 Tithe Map extract, which identifies the dates and locations of the four Town Halls. In addition, for consistency, the words 'Old Tolsey' and 'Tolsey' refer to the First and Second Town Halls respectively.

The first record is a 1439 lease of part of the Second Town Hall in Market Place – the one that became known as the Tolsey. The Mayor and Burgesses let the messuage (meaning a dwelling in its curtilage) part of it to Richard Hamond and his wife Alice for the longer of their two lives. That part of 'Le Tolsyde' in use as a shop and known as 'Le Stokhous', was not included in the lease. It seems that the Tolsey was a building located in Market Place, at the junction of High Street, Church Street and Castle Street. This is because the next lease, in the batch of records called the Market Place Series, was dated 1491 and referred to property in the Market Place 'next to the house called Le Tolseyle'. Hence, the Tolsey appears to have been a house in 1491. It might well be asked why the Corporation were leasing out their Town Hall in 1439 for domestic and retail purposes. It is possible that the tenants were responsible for market matters and made available the main room for the Mayor and Burgesses when needed. But since we cannot now be sure about it, it is not definite that the Tolsey had become the Town Hall by 1439 or 1491. At those dates, the Town Hall could still have been the Old Tolsey.

In contrast to the earlier documents, a 40-year lease from Michaelmas 1497 paints a different picture. In a letting to John Tuls of Holnehurst, land is described as follows: 'a plot of land lying between two columns to the west of the Town Hall, formerly the "Tollsell" with 2½ feet of land to the east in front of the two columns over which the Town Hall is built.' Another translation from the Latin reads: 'Piece of land lying between two holdings on west of the common house of the Borough called the Town Hall, otherwise the Tolsell, with 2½ feet of land towards the east in front of these holdings with the Town Hall built above.' We can take it that a 'holding' meant an upright support or column. A condition of the lease, granted for two shillings a year, was that the tenant had to enclose the land and build a structure on it with doors and windows in the form of a shop.

Fig.2

Current Building on the Old Tolsey site,
now occupied by The Carphone Warehouse

Rather like the Third Town Hall, this one, the First Town Hall, appears to have been built on a road, Millhams Street. The building was leased out after the Corporation relocated to the Second Town Hall in probably the fifteenth century. Unfortunately, the appearance and structure of the Old Tolsey, demolished by 1788, is not now known.

By 1497 therefore, during the reign of Henry VII, we are being told that the Tolsey has changed from being a house to being the Town Hall, although it would be very difficult to produce a sketch of the demised premises from this description. But what does seem fairly clear is that the

Town Hall was above the ground level shop just before the end of the 15th century. The description in this lease is also an indication in favour of the Tolsey being in accord with the market halls of the era, i.e. with open or partly open ground levels and a first floor chamber as sketched in *Fig.4*. It follows that the Old Tolsey was by then probably no longer used as the Town Hall.

In 1572, the 'Old Tolsye' was let by the Corporation to William Nutkyn, a tanner. Putting it all together, it is reasonably clear that a Town Hall, known as the Tolsey, existed by 1497 at the Market Place and the Old Tolsey was being leased out as surplus to Corporation needs in the 16th century.

After it had ceased to be used by the Corporation, the Old Tolsey was converted wholly or partly to residential accommodation. It could well have been this original building as converted and maintained over the years, which lasted until its poor condition required demolition and redevelopment in 1788. Assuming that to be so, it means that the townspeople would have seen their oldest Council Chamber surviving for some 42 years after the demolition of the newer one, the Tolsey, in 1746. No doubt this would have been an opportunity for the oldest inhabitant to remark that 'they don't build Town Halls like they used to!'

Fig.2 shows the present building on the corner of High Street and Millhams Street. *Fig.3* is a photograph from about 1885 of the same building. As a site with limited prominence, narrow frontage and considerable depth, it is a little odd that it was used as a Market House. The same cannot be said of the Second Town Hall site, that of the Tolsey.

Following the 1788 demolition, a new house was built and later sold in 1823 to Henry Ginn – according to the 1841 Census, his family were still in occupation. They included Martha Ginn, School Mistress (50), Mary Ginn, Milliner (25), Martha Ginn (16) and Mary Ann Shelton, Apprentice (18). In 1823 (and for that matter in 1841), all may have seemed to be well. A natural residential redevelopment, with some retail use, had taken place in 1788 due to the previous ancient building being at the end of its physical life. But this was far from the case. By 1826, Henry was in financial difficulty being unable to raise a much-needed mortgage on what was by then called Tolsey House. The vendor, of the interest sold to him three years earlier, was a Burgess of Christchurch. However, since the only title available to Henry Ginn was a lease from 1788, it meant that such title was somewhat defective. It was not exactly a fee simple that would have been a proper security for a mortgage – Mr. Ginn's potential lender was of course worried about the Council reclaiming the house. Now we have the Land Registry, which provides Copy Certificates that give a state guarantee of title for the benefit of buyers. In those early times, a legal advisor had more difficulty and responsibility in exercising the 'art of conveyancing' and advising the client.

As a consequence of the title defect, quite properly and understandably, Mr. Ginn had been given a bond by the vendor, i.e. an indemnity that he would have quiet enjoyment. He now required that the Corporation either say they wanted to recover possession so that he might claim under his bond, or agree to leave him unmolested so that he might secure his mortgage. Faced with a need to respond to the occupier's letter and strong reminders, the Corporation sought counsel's opinion. In the end, the legal advice received did not favour the position of the Corporation in any possible attempt to recover their property. Thus we have the extraordinary situation of the town 'losing' its first Town Hall due to the neglect or worse of the Mayors and Burgesses of the 18th century and the early 19th century.

In order to answer Mr. Ginn, the Corporation had to give counsel the full background. Before coming to this however, it is worth noting the use and occupation of the Old Tolsey in previous centuries – times when ownership was successfully retained. There were various leases of the Old Tolsey by the Mayor and Burgesses (acting as landlords) after it was no longer the Town Hall:

24.11.1572	William Jerman to William Nutkyn, tanner, for 19 years at 12d. p.a.
24.10.1591	John Nutkyn to John Clare, for 21 years at 2s. p.a. and 40s. consideration.
1612	William Colgill to John Woodnot, mercer for life of Woodnot and Joane his daughter, for 2s. p.a. and 30s. consideration. (The record actually says for the life of Colgill and Joane Woodnot his daughter. However, it is here presumed to mean Joane Woodnot was John Woodnot's daughter, not the Mayor's daughter.)
10.3.1636/7	John Hildesley to John Woodnot, clerk for 20 years at 2s. p.a. and consideration £3.
2.11.1664	Henry Rogers to William Collins, shoemaker for 21 years from 10.6.1670 at 2s. p.a. and consideration 4 of 40s.
8.7.1696	James Stevens to John Burden, brazier for 99 years at 2s. 6d. p.a. and consideration 12d.

On two occasions, a letting was to a future or past Mayor, i.e. William Nutkyn and John Clare.

The Corporation's research in 1826 showed that the problem began with a lease to James Collens from 1716 of the 'messuage, tenement and dwelling house, sometime called Old Tolsey' for the shorter of 99 years and the life of his niece Catherine Rolph (later Dorey) at 2 shillings per annum. The Collens will of 1737 bequeathed to his friends William Blake, John Cook and James Stevens the yearly profits of the property, it then being occupied by William Yandell, although Catherine still lived. Three years later, the three friends conveyed their full interest to Catherine, by now a widow, in respect of the remainder of the 99 years and her life. She is not believed to have died until around 1796; the date occupation should have been given back to the Corporation as freeholders.

Fig.3

**Building erected on the site of the Old Tolsey,
about 100 years after its demolition**
(Reproduced by courtesy of Red House Museum, Christchurch)

Believed to date from about 1885, this is the same building as in Fig.2 but then occupied by a boot and shoe warehouse. Although the site had last been used for a Town Hall some 400 years before the photograph was taken, it was still in the days of the horse and cart. By 1885, less than 60 years had passed since the ownership of the land had been wrested from the Corporation by adverse possession.

Although therefore Catherine was still alive in 1788, it appears that a ground lease was then granted by Rebecca Jeans, widow of Joshua Jeans, to Mary Ginn. Rebecca had been the occupier of the relentlessly deteriorating

Old Tolsey building, which was described as being in a ruinous state and taken down that year. It might here be mentioned that Joshua Jeans, three times Mayor of Christchurch, was the corrupt Supervisor of Riding Officers, responsible for combating smuggling. Instead, he actively supported the so-called Free Traders culminating in the Battle of Mudeford 1784. He was dismissed from his job as untrustworthy in May 1786 and died a broken man some six months later.

How could the recent widow Rebecca grant any such lease when Catherine was the Corporation's tenant? Yet the document refers specifically to it as Rebecca's property: 'all that the site or piece or parcel of land whereon stood lately a messuage or tenement of the said Rebecca Jeans.' The implication is that Rebecca was the last occupier of the Old Tolsey before demolition. Since she was related to James Stevens, one of the beneficiaries under the 1737 will, the Council thought that she may have been under the impression it belonged to him, although he knew it was Council property. The records do not explain how that theory meant she felt able to grant a ground lease!

We are now looking at the cleared site of 1788. As new ground tenant, Mary Ginn proceeded to build a brick messuage or tenement. She took it for 35 years at £2. 2s. 0d. per annum, thereby expiring in the year that Henry Ginn purportedly bought the property from a Burgess. Hence, in 1823, it seems that the Burgess, acting as a representative of Rebecca Jeans, provided this expired lease as the only title to the property on its sale to Henry Ginn.

The road boundaries, of the land given in the 1788 ground lease, are described (in the Corporation's request for counsel's opinion) together with its position adjoining the Ship Inn. Overall dimensions are given of 17 feet by 70 feet. Since this is such an important historical site, dating back to the 15th century and probably earlier, it was well worth checking these figures. I duly found an average depth of 70 feet 6 inches and rear brickwork width of 15 feet 3 inches, widening to about 16 feet 3 inches when allowing for a slight change in direction in the north-west flank wall. Allowing further (as one should) for the corbelled eaves courses, it becomes approximately 16 feet 11 inches. The High Street frontage is 17 feet, again reflecting the eaves. The measurements taken on the ground could scarcely be closer to those provided in the 1788 lease. Moreover, it is almost certain that the Carphone Warehouse building in *Fig.2* is the one erected for Mary Ginn at that time.

Clearly, the feeling in 1826 was that the property management history of the Old Tolsey site was most improper – counsel was even told all Burgesses were under oath not to embezzle or conceal Corporation property. For good measure, his opinion was also sought concerning other Christchurch property, where no rent had been paid for many years and adverse possession had seemingly succeeded at the expense of the town. The ensuing legal view was that it was unsafe for the Council to proceed to try title by ejectment, when there had indeed been adverse possession of the Old Tolsey land for over twenty years. Beyond this, a writ of right was considered very problematical and in any case, an action of the Corporation could be barred due to non-claim for more than five years.

Fig.4

Typical Town Hall which may be like the Tolsey
(Second Town Hall)
(Reproduced by courtesy of the Christchurch Local History Society)

This sketch first appeared in a book by local historian Allen White in 1982. It is similar to the restored Town Hall in Fig.5 and typical of the period. The first floor Council Chamber was where the Mayor and Burgesses met to take their decisions whilst the open ground level section was for market use. No original drawings of the actual Christchurch Tolsey appear to have survived.

Reverting to Henry Ginn, a seemingly innocent party in the matter, he was certainly most anxious to resolve the matter and having some difficulty in getting a response from a reluctant Corporation. To quote his reminder letter of 12th February 1827: '... not yet having been informed if the claim has been decided, I again trouble you with this ... makes it <u>very injurious</u> to me, and am unable to mortgage which puts me to a considerable inconvenience. I therefore must respectfully solicit your early attention thereto, either to <u>enforce</u> or <u>relinquish</u> the said claim ...' The answer to him must have been that the Corporation had no plans to enforce their rights of ownership. In line with this, the Ginn family were still in occupation as we have seen at the time of the 1841 Census. In the same year, on 20 March 1841, the Corporation took the rare step of reckoning up their total annual income for all their property, finding it to be £67. 7s. only. The house built on the site of the Old Tolsey is not on that property schedule. In further confirmation (as at the time of writing in 2009), the Council have advised that they now have no remaining interest in the Old Tolsey land.

The property management history of the Old Tolsey site had come to an end. More than 300 years after the time when the Old Tolsey had been replaced, Christchurch lost its ownership of the freehold interest in the site of its first Town Hall through adverse possession, commonly known as squatters' title. We may not know much about what the Old Tolsey looked like or even whether it was a two storey or single storey building. Nor can we say after all this time much about what was decided there. Despite this, it remains important as the beginning of Christchurch local government and an early example of public property ownership on behalf of the inhabitants.

CHAPTER TWO

FIFTEENTH CENTURY AND A NEW HALL

For the next period until about 1746, the Mayor and Burgesses ran the town from the Tolsey at Market Place, also known as Market Square. It was evidently decided that the Old Tolsey had outrun its usefulness and it was time for a change and relocation to the irregularly-shaped junction of three roads – Church Street, Castle Street and High Street. In that respect, the Tolsey (the Second Town Hall) was the same as its famous, slightly earlier contemporary the Guildhall at Thaxted, also built at the junction of three roads. Furthermore, since Councils have always upgraded, the Tolsey was no doubt an improvement on the Old Tolsey, even though the evidence from the old leases is that it was a conversion from a house. The main improvement may have simply been prominence of position.

The requirement of the time was evidently to have a first floor meeting room approached from a landing that might be open-sided and having the area below for market use. The Tolsey was certainly in a much better spot than its predecessor to observe market activity and uphold the law. Market days and fairs were highly popular and profitable with much more ale consumed in town than on a normal day. No doubt the Corporation-appointed Ale Taster would have been kept busy with the 'leather breeches test' – if the ale was impure with too much sugar, it would cause him to stick fast to a bench on which it was poured! At some risk of digression, properly brewed ale would have virtually no sugar left as it would have been converted to alcohol by correct fermentation. It would also have been very easy for anyone to address people from the landing – a perceived disadvantage perhaps at a later time, because the feature was 'designed out' of the Third Town Hall.

It is best to be as clear as possible about the uncertain provenance of the 'Tolsey likeness' in *Fig.4*. It was dated 1982 and appeared in a book by local historian Allen White. However, the restored market hall, which he mentions in connection with it, is the one now standing at the Weald and Downland Open Air Museum at Singleton near Chichester. That was transferred from Titchfield and has been carefully dated to 1619. Although *Fig.5* shows the restoration as somewhat different from the sketch, the Curator of the Weald and Downland considers it to be the same building. The safest thing to say is that these two pictures only give a general idea of the Second Town Hall of Christchurch, i.e. they are typical of the period for a small market town. At least some old leases of premises at or by the Tolsey in the Market Place are described in a way consistent with this idea. For instance, the columns of the Town Hall at ground level may be referred to in the document. If any reader has more information about the exact appearance of the Tolsey, we would be delighted to hear about it at the Christchurch Local History Society.

Fig.5

Present-day restoration of Tichfield Town Hall
(Copyright of the Weald and Downland Open Air Museum)

Here is a rescued former Town Hall, or it could also be called a Market Hall. It has been accurately dated by dendrochronology to 1619 and now on display at Singleton, near Chichester. Although it was built much later than the Christchurch Tolsey, the building style of such Market Halls did not change very much. It follows that our Second Town Hall, the Tolsey, could well have looked rather like this. A difference is that the lock-up (or prison cell) shown under the stairs did not appear in the Tolsey certainly after 1582, because by then a lease states that there was a nearby building called the Blind House used as the Town Prison.

The Tolsey lasted for well over 300 years. It seems to have been originally a house and later inextricably linked with trades-people, particularly butchers, who occupied parts of it on a series of leases. In those days of a much smaller Christchurch, the real town centre was probably at or near this spot, because it was a road intersection giving access to the all-important Priory Church, the bridges over the River Avon leading to the east and the market itself. In comparison, development was less concentrated towards the north-west end of the High Street. For example, even as late as the Tithe Map of 1843, the large site in the High Street, known as Blanchard's Yard (now at Saxon Square), was merely a meadow running from the road to the Mill Stream. In one way, there was a parallel with the previous hall – they were both built in the road. Whilst the first one was a rectangular incursion into Millhams Street, this one was erected on what is now a road tarmac surface (*Fig.1*)! The same might be said of its replacement the Third Town Hall.

Decisions would have been taken in the first floor chamber. The Mayor and Burgesses would have met at the appointed hour, climbed the steps to where they would have had a good view of the town and proceeded to discuss the matters requiring resolutions. Just like Council committees today, there were often adjournments since they had insufficient information. One regular function was to elect to office Mayor, Constables, Bailiffs, Ale Taster and Hayward, who was responsible for repairs to fences and ditches. When necessary, a legal opinion or some building estimates would be sought. Sometimes, the Mayor, or a small sub-committee including him and perhaps two Burgesses, would be formed to carry out a resolution as they thought fit. In addition, the market needed administering and property needed managing. It may be fair to say that the job of the Corporation has always been to adapt as needed to look after the interests of the townspeople. To a large extent in the early days, that meant using these officials to maintain the law.

At a time when Christchurch Town Hall was the Tolsey, a 16th century appreciation of the nature of civic duty was laid down in the minutes as almost a Frontispiece (*Fig.6*). It is a sort of dedication by Burgess Thomas Hancock to the Mayor, his brethren the other Burgesses and the Commoners of the Borough. Perhaps it was best coming from a Burgess. In modern management-speak, we might call it the 'Council's vision statement'. It can be seen that he felt long life, health and happiness should be the lot of the town and its leaders – a wise aspiration of the Corporation to act for the benefit of the people of Christchurch.

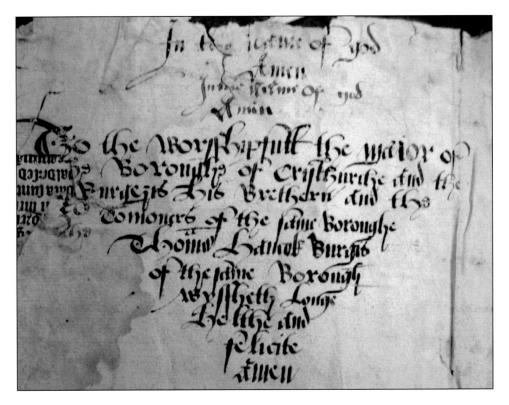

Fig.6

Dedication of the Old Minute Book

(Reproduced by courtesy of Dorset History Centre Ref. DC/CC/Acc 7982 Box 9)

Thomas Hancock, Mayor of the Corporation in 1556, 1561 and 1573 had this dedication inserted at the front of the Old Minute Book when he was a Burgess. The transcription reads as follows:

>In the name of god
>Amen
>In the name of god
>Amin
>
>To the Worsshipful the maior of
>The Boroughe of Cristchurche And the
>Burgeses his Brethren And the
>Comoners of the same Boroughe
>Thomas Hacok Burgis
>Of the same Borough
>Wyssheth Longe [life]
>Helthe And
>Felicite
>Amen

Town records were kept in a large book with a typical meeting resulting in one hand-written page (using black ink) that ended with any resolutions and the signatures of all members. Provided you could read the writing, it was all very simple. Money was very limited with a big reliance on very modest incoming rents, subscriptions and a regular need to cut or remove altogether the Mayor's allowance. In line with the long-term severe financial restriction, Corporation powers were not great. Indeed, for hundreds of years, it was appropriate to limit the work of the Borough. By comparison, its amount of work today is enormous – a direct reflection of our relative prosperity. The Dissolution of the monasteries took place during the time of the Tolsey in 1539. A description of the town by Prior Draper was very revealing, even though he was painting something of a picture in order to make a case to King Henry VIII for leniency. He refers to the poor town of Christchurch, set in a desolate place in a little corner of the realm with many of the inhabitants relieved with bread and ale from the Priory.

An impression can be gained of local government at the Tolsey by reviewing some of the deliberations of the era. Many were of routine nature, being concerned with the election of Mayors, the administration of oaths and general property management such as repairs and leasing. Some instances are given below.

In 1517 and 1557, 40-year and 41-year shop leases were granted respectively of part of the Tolsey itself. The first described it as 'a shop next to the Cross in the Market Place between the eastern columns'. The second lease was for the same property and had a tenant's repairing covenant 'including part of the Tolsell, which is over the shop'. The leases prove that (at least in most of the 16th century) the ground level of the Tolsey was not fully open for the benefit of stalls on market days.

By an indenture from September 1582, the members let premises to a butcher William Peeters: 'one shope sett lying and beinge in the markett place adioyninge to the new prison in the boroughe afore sayde...' The 21 year lease was on a full repairing basis. It was spelt out that it had to be delivered up to the Mayor and Burgesses at the end of the lease in good condition and any repairs notified by the landlords would have to be done inside 20 days. Failing compliance with the notification in the stated time, the landlords would have the right of re-entry. In short, this was a proper and professionally prepared lease.

A further 40-year lease in 1600, to a glover, identified the shop being let as 'under the Market House'. In 1641, a 21 year lease was granted to a butcher of two shops lately converted to one shop under the west end of the

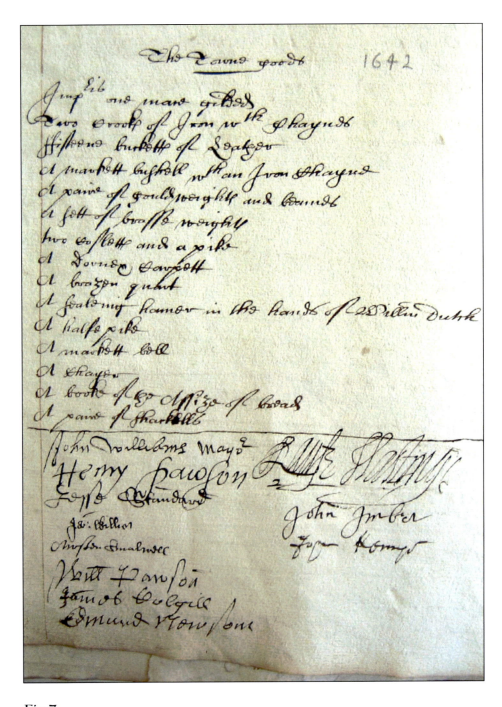

Fig.7

Town Goods of Christchurch
(Reproduced by courtesy of Dorset History Centre Ref. DC/CC/Acc 7982 Box 9)

Town Hall. All in all, we can safely say that the Tolsey was a mixed-use building – Market House and Town Hall.

On a regular basis, a record was kept of the items held by the Corporation, it was a simple stock-take in order to keep track and avoid losses. The transcription of this example shown on the opposite page from 1642 reads as follows (with some comments in brackets):

Imprimis one mace gilded	(Imprimis meaning in the first place)
Two Crookes of Iron w[i]th Chaynes	
Fifteene buckettes of Leather	
A markett bushel w[i]th Iron Chayne	(Container of this capacity, about 35 litres)
A paire of gould weights and beames	
A sett of brasse weightes	
Two Coslettes and a pike	
A Doune?? & Carpett	
A brazen quart	(Brass container of this capacity)
A sealeing hamer in the hands of Will[ia]m Dutch	
	(Probably an implement to seal official documents)
A halfe pike	(Shafted weapon having a pointed blade and crossbar at its base, as used by 17th century infantry officers)
A markett bell	
A Chager	
A book of the Assize of bread	
A paire of shackells	

It was considered important for the Mayor and Burgesses to take oaths and to regularly sign off the Town Goods. In 1616, they comprised the newly made silver mace (cost £4. 15s. 6d.), two crooks and 15 leather buckets. In 1620, they included a mace of silver parcel gilt, two town crooks, the market bell and 'weights and scales to weigh bread'. By 1642, the Town Goods had expanded as set out in the records shown in *Fig.7*. There is a real and tangible historical link to be seen in the mace, as shown in *Fig.8*. It has survived the centuries as the symbol of the Borough's continuing powers and is still used for ceremonial purposes. The inscription HENRY HASTINGS (Mayor 1662) remains very clear.

Around 1637, the Privy Council were sent a petition by Arundel of Wardour, the Lord of the Manor of Christchurch that John Hildesley was wrongly elected as Mayor. The Court Leet had found him ineligible, acquiring the mace from the old Mayor by 'indirect practice', also, living as he did outside the Borough and rarely visiting it. Not to be outdone, the Inhabitants and Commonalty of the Borough sent their own petition to the

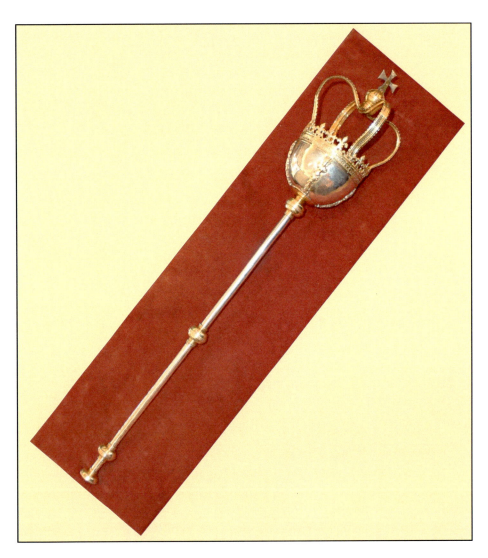

Fig.8

First Mace of the Corporation
(Reproduced by courtesy of Christchurch Borough Council)

There was some historical debate about the provenance of the Mace being before or after the Civil War. An earlier story has it that the Mace was sent to Southampton Castle for safe-keeping but it was never returned afterwards. Accordingly, the one in the picture was believed to have been supplied by Henry Hastings who was Mayor in 1662 and has his name inscribed on the bottom knob. However, the generally accepted current view (based on research by local historians Arthur Lloyd and Allen White) is that the Borough still has the original 1616 Mace, because it was indeed returned in 1658. Hence, the Mayor's name merely signifies repairs to it during his term of office. (There is also a second Mace, it was presented by the Military Engineering and Experimental Establishment in 1969.)

Privy Council saying he had been peaceably elected, the mace had been delivered to him by the previous Mayor in the normal way and he was indeed a resident of the parish and a frequent visitor. They further responded to complain that the steward of the Lord of the Manor had refused to administer the oath to their elected bailiff. In 1639, Arundel died leaving a last-minute will and a long-running legal dispute wherein his six daughters had to fight for their inheritance. However that may be, Hildesley remains listed as one of the official Mayors of the town!

In 1651, the Corporation made an agreement (for one year renewable) with bricklayer John Wylde, allowing him to dig clay and burn bricks on common land. For his part, Wylde agreed to sell good, hard and well-burnt bricks to the Inhabitants at nine shillings per thousand. For three whole days after the kiln was broken, the Christchurch Inhabitants were to have the exclusive right of purchase of his bricks.

In 1662, concerns had arisen about what was happening to the funds of the Borough – it was felt by many to be quite wrong for the 'town's profits' to be shared among the Burgesses. An agreement was reached that in future these should be used as should be judged most fit by the Mayor and the majority part of the Burgesses. Henry Hastings, the Mayor, signed this together with 92 others!

In 1665, the members had to debate the plague – a chilling pointer to the hardships of the times. It was ordered that a constant watch and ward was to be kept day and night for the better preservation of the Town against plague and pestilence. No men coming from London were to be admitted to the Town for 20 days.

In September 1718, there was evidently a dispute between the Mayor and Burgesses. As a result, it was resolved that the Mayor was not to be allowed to swear in any Burgess unless the consent was first obtained of the major part of the Burgesses residing in the Borough. The out-Burgesses of Christchurch were not to be included in this scheme. The penalty for non-compliance was set at the enormous sum of £100.

Burgesses were involved in electing members for Parliament in these days when Christchurch was a 'pocket' or 'rotten' Borough returning two members. The Boroughs were so called due to being 'in the pocket' of the main landowner. For instance, the Mayor and Burgesses were unlikely to debate too seriously the idea of electing anyone other than Sir Peter Mews, who was Lord of the Manor and M.P. at the start of the 18th century. Perhaps it was all somewhat too 'cosy'. In even earlier times (1643), it was ordered that no man be elected Burgess for Parliament unless he was first sworn in as Burgess for the Borough according to ancient custom.

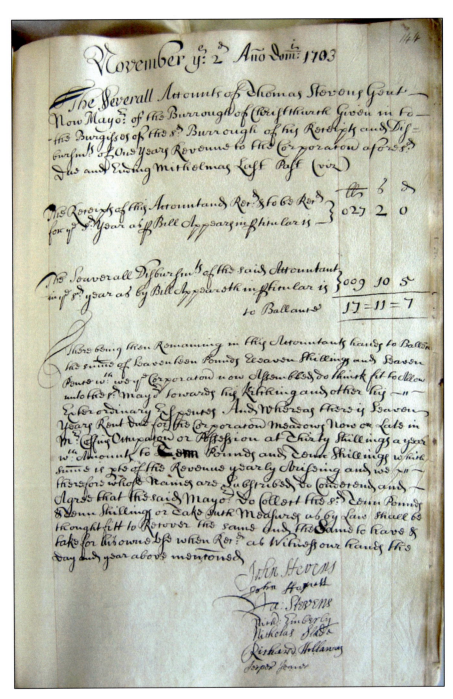

Fig.9

Corporation Accounts from November 1703

(Reproduced by courtesy of Dorset History Centre Ref.DC/CC/Acc 7982 Box 9)

Referring to the Victoria County History, in 1832 there were 35 Burgesses, of whom only 20 at most had ever voted in the preceding 30 years to elect a member to Parliament – and the franchise was restricted to the Corporation only! The same situation would have applied to the days of the Tolsey being the Town Hall. For instance, the town records show that a return was made on 9th May 1741 with the following information:

> Return recording the election of Charles Ormond Powlet and Edward Hooper, junior, Esqs., Burgesses as M.P.'s, following precept issued by Rumney Diggle, Esq., Sheriff of Hampshire, following dissolution of Parliament. Rober Dale, LL.D., was Mayor of Christchurch. Next session of Parliament to begin on 25 June 1741.

In 1703, the accounts were presented to the members of the Corporation and approved as shown in *Fig.9*. They are included in order to give an idea of the very limited nature of early local government. Here we have a year's spending, as managed by the Mayor and Burgesses amounting to £9. 10s. 5d. However, some rent was unpaid and remedial measures were required, as shown by the following transcription when our language was at an earlier stage:

> There being then Remaining in this Accountants hands to Balance the sum of Seventeen Pounds Eleven Shillings and Seven Pence which we the Corporation here Assembled do think fit to Allow unto the Mayor towards his Kilching and other his Extraordinary Expenses. And whereas there is Seven Years Rent due for the Corporation Meadows Now or Later in Mr. Coffin's Occupation or Possession at Thirty Shillings a year which Amounts to Ten Pounds Ten Shillings which sum is parte of the Revenue yearly Arising and we therefore whose Names are Subscribed do Condescend and Agree that the said Mayor Do Collect these Ten Pounds and Ten Shillings or take such Measures as by law shall be thought fit to Recover the same and the Same to have and take for his own Use when Received as Witness our hands the day and year above mentioned.

More generally, it is an example of the good decision-making process. The members clearly discussed the best way forward in any particular case and reached a conclusion that was put in the minutes and nearly always signed by all present. Since the minute book was used for literally hundreds of years, there would have been proper continuity and no trouble locating previous resolutions. Even the simplicity of the available writing implements exercised a strict discipline – there was no waffle at all!

These few instances from local history have been included to show how the Town Hall was a real part of town life. After all, in the same way as a church, the work carried on and the people who do that are more important than the actual building.

Fig.10

Third Town Hall at the end of Castle Street
(Reproduced by courtesy of the Red House Museum, Christchurch)

A photograph of an etching done about 1840 by Benjamin Ferrey and presumably now in a private collection. The hall can be seen to be obstructing the road quite severely and this picture alone shows why the Corporation tried to obtain land to its left in order to allow the traffic to be safer. The hotel on the right, named Humby's, is now the Kings Hotel.

CHAPTER THREE

THIRD TOWN HALL IN MID-STREET

In around 1746, a much better two-storey building was erected in the same general location as the Tolsey, including a first floor chamber and an open-arched market area below (*Fig.10*). According to the 1920 *Reminiscences* of J.P. and five times ex-Mayor of Christchurch, William Tucker, houses and shambles (a word meaning slaughterhouse) were demolished at that time to help provide the site for the works. Clearly, this particular information derives from his great knowledge of the town rather than personal experience. It was a continuation to a higher standard of the local government facility, already established nearby. Since no accurate maps go back to earlier than 1746, we cannot say exactly how the road layout changed with the building of the Third Town Hall. If it replaced houses, a slaughterhouse and the Tolsey, it seems to have been a major upgrade of Corporation premises. In spite of its quality compared to the previous building, it was destined to last for a much shorter time. Demolition was in 1859, followed in 1860 by the completion of the Fourth Town Hall in the High Street, with an enclosed ground floor and large rear extension. Records of the building job of 1746 survive to some extent.

Incidentally, although this book refers to 1746 for the time when the Town Hall was built, that is for convenience and the work continued up to 1748. For instance, Mr. Percy submitted a bill for £5. 5s. for work done in June 1747 – for this sum, there was carriage and delivery of 'a chimney piece stone work' and the setting was done. Regarding the main construction job, an account exists to show that the members gave much more than was needed.

An account of the moneys received and paid by the late Mayor Mr. Samuel Roy towards the building the Markett House and the Town Hall.

Received from the members of the moneys by them given for the erecting the above building the sum of   315: 0: 0

A schedule follows of payments to many tradesmen totalling   225: 3: 2

Remain of the 315 and accounted for to the members who have given)
and delivered the same into the hands of the present Mayor to   )   89:16:10
discharge the remaining demands on account of the said building   )
                                                                                    315: 0: 0

(Extract reproduced by courtesy of the Dorset History Centre Ref. DC/CC/C/5/2/14)

Fig.11

High Street celebration of the Reform Act 1832
(Reproduced by courtesy of the Red House Museum, Christchurch)

According to the drawing, on 25 July in that year, each person was provided with a plate, a cup and a knife and fork. Since the Act was the start of the process towards universal suffrage, it was well worthy of celebration on such a massive scale. The bell tower of the Third Town Hall can be seen as can its two arches facing west.

Thus, for well over 100 years up to 1859, Christchurch had the doubtful benefit of a Town Hall situated at an increasingly busy road junction with traffic on three sides. Following its demolition, the whole site was taken into the road – hence the chapter heading. Today, it is hard to credit a two-storey building in that spot and having a 46-foot flank wall running roughly from the mini-roundabout and along the middle of Castle Street! The other flank wall left just a few feet for pedestrians only. Admittedly, we are going back to the middle of the 18th century, when everything was based on horses, carts and carriages, and a forecast of the internal combustion engine would have been met with frank disbelief. Yet, although the town was also much smaller than now, so generating much less movement, it can be seen from *Fig.10* just how badly it was placed. In one way however, it was well placed – long poles with iron hooks were kept hung up under the Town Hall for use in pulling off thatch from buildings on fire!

Fig.11 shows a broadly recognisable High Street including the Third Town Hall. In 1832, there was evidently an enormous High Street celebration of the increase in suffrage arising from the Reform Act of that year. Although this painting shows the building from quite a distance, it can still be recognised from the arches and bell tower. The general impression of affluence given by the picture may be more favourable than the reality. For example, the Boundary Commissioners of 1832 reported that no trade or manufactures were then carried on. In addition they noted: 'The town presents no symptoms of activity or industry. The houses are of a middling description. The appearance of the inhabitants, who are thinly scattered, gives no indications of prosperity.' Another illustration of the poor situation within Castle Street (*Fig.12*) is possibly the most well-known of all – a view from the south side of the High Street at a moment of low traffic.

In passing, it is worth noting that the road layout problem was largely caused by the Normans. Before the castle was built, Wick Lane continued straight into what is now Castle Street without deviation, as did High Street into Church Street – it was a normal crossroads. The curtilage needs of the castle and moat pushed both roads out of line – Church Street a bit to the west and Castle Street a bit to the north. The shifting of the latter gave us the staggered junction we have today. Without this slightly higgledy-piggledy road system caused by the building decisions for Christchurch Castle, a Town Hall might never have been erected on what was really road land.

Fig.12

Most detailed view existing of the Third Town Hall
(Reproduced by courtesy of the Red House Museum, Christchurch)

This photograph of an etching, believed to date from 1830 to 1840, is so clear that today's 'Mayor's Parlour' can easily be recognised from it. Since it is known that the width of the building was 20 feet, the artist, Benjamin Ferrey, may have used some artistic licence. This is because the distance from the furthest visible corner of the hall to the building on the left was less than 20 feet on the ground, yet it seems in the view shown to be greater than the hall width. John Lewis at the Museum considers it possible that Ferrey produced the etching from an existing painting.

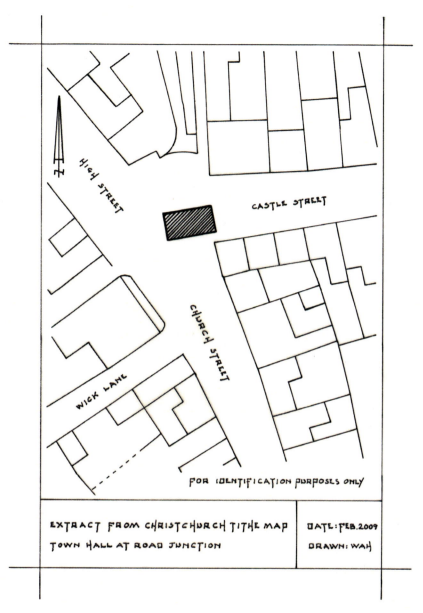

Fig.13
Setting of the 1746 Town Hall based on the 1843 Tithe Map

The author's drawing is necessarily somewhat diagrammatic and no attempt should be made to scale from it. The version used as a basis was that on display in the Priory Church. However, the two other versions seen have slight differences – such maps are not of the same quality as those by the Ordnance Survey. For example, the main side walls are shown as shorter than they were on the ground. Suffice it to say that with the north-west corner of the building, being close to today's mini-roundabout, the setting was awkward.

Fig.13 is my drawing of the junction of the three roads and buildings nearby. It repeats as faithfully as possible, to a larger scale, part of the somewhat indistinct Christchurch Tithe Map, now on display in St. Michael's Loft at the Priory Church. At least two other Tithe Maps exist and are very slightly different. These maps, although fairly clear, are not quite as accurate as Ordnance Survey ones and, like *Fig.13*, are more for identification only. For example, although the actual building was relatively longer than shown in *Fig.13*, it is best to repeat the historical document as closely as possible, rather than try to 'improve' on it.

Taking account of the maps and other information available, the position of the north-west corner of the Third Town Hall was determined. For the photograph in *Fig.14*, the ex-Mayors were placed at all four corners of the former building and one, Mrs. Fox, in the middle of one side wall. Although the location of the north-west corner is only accurate to about a yard in the author's view, at least the picture amply demonstrates the awkwardness of the road junction until the 1859 demolition. As for the accuracy of the other three corners, the siting of the ex-Mayors is broadly consistent with the Tithe Map. The same is true regarding a comment from William Tucker. His *Reminiscences* mention that 'the carriageway between Town Hall pavement at Lloyds Bank was only about 12 to 14 ft.'

But what is known of the life of the Town Hall? What happened there and why? We saw in the last chapter something of the decisions and resolutions then exercising the Corporation. Again, within the very limited scope of this sort of book, a few examples must now suffice.

There was much lively debate in the approach to the Reform Act of 1832. Many 'pocket' Boroughs were abolished and elsewhere new constituencies created more in line with areas of population. In the case of Christchurch, the office of one of its two elected members was abolished. Certainly, it was described in minutes as a period of great popular excitement and unprovoked aggression. The cause was felt to be twofold – the protracted discussion and the subsequent enactment. Thanks were duly awarded by the Burgesses to Mayor John Spicer for his 'temperate and judicious conduct'. Presumably, he successfully used the force of his office and his personality to keep the peace against the consequences of too much drink.

On 18th December 1833, a major discussion took place to do with civic dignity and robes. The result was a resolution to revive the ancient practice of proper attire for civic occasions – the custom described in a minute of 25th January 1641 was to be renewed. The Burgesses were given just days to fit themselves out with dark blue cloth faced in black velvet to a pattern still to be fixed, and all in time for Christmas! These robes were to be worn at every public hall and also when the Mayor was being accompanied to Church every Christmas Day, Easter Sunday and Whit Sunday. In addition, the Mayor and ex-Mayors were to wear a scarlet scarf trimmed with fur or ermine (or it may mean fur of ermine, i.e. the white fur of a stoat valued as a symbol of high rank). The order of precedence in all processions was also spelt out – Mayor and ex Mayor first, followed by previous Mayors strictly in accord with their 'priority in serving the Office of Mayor'. Unusually, the entry is in the form of a memorandum inserted into the Minute Book and signed only by the Mayor Arthur Quartley 'on behalf of the meeting'. One can imagine that the Burgesses delegated that task to him, whilst they rushed off to place their orders for new robes!

On 24th July 1837, nominations were made for Sir George Henry Rose and William Gordon to be considered for Parliament. The next day the votes were recorded as 116 for Rose compared to 105 for Gordon, giving a majority of 11 to Rose, so securing the seat for him as minuted by the Mayor, still Arthur Quartley. Although the electorate sounds extremely small, it was much larger than applicable before the 1832 Reform Act under which the Mayor and Burgesses alone put forward a member from their number.

On 14th September 1848, there was a riot connected with the Port Field. Two days later, the Corporation resolved that the Mayor and Town Clerk would next confer with the other proprietors and occupiers who were injured and take such measures for the punishment of the offenders as were calculated to prevent a repetition of such outrages. At a review on 22nd September, Druitt proposed indictments should be preferred against the offenders in concert with other injured parties. However, Burgesses Goddard and Collins proposed the matter be 'passed over' and instead, the Inhabitants be consulted with a view to enclosing Port Field, thereby preventing a recurrence. The voting was six to two in favour of indictments and against the matter being 'passed over'.

The office of Town Clerk is the predecessor of a council's Chief Executive today. Moreover, as local government expanded gaining various Chief Officers and their deputies, the Town Clerk, generally a qualified solicitor, was the acknowledged boss amongst the others. In 1840, the salary of the Corporation's Town Clerk was set at £5 annually. The same year, James Druitt was sworn in as Deputy Town Clerk and in 1846 elected and sworn in as Town Clerk. As a very able solicitor and property dealer, he was a major asset to the town in carrying through the relocation project of 1859 to 1860.

Fig.14

Position of the Third Town Hall marked by five ex-Mayors

Particular thanks are due to the ex-Mayors for agreeing to stand at 7 a.m. on a Sunday morning where the four corners of the building (and the centre of one long side) have now been hidden under tarmac. They are, with their dates of mayoralty service, as follows: Michael Hodges (1978), Mrs. Norma Fox (1985), Michael Winfield (1986), David Fox (1987 & 2006) and Edward Coope (1994). The corners were fixed by creating a scale from a long measurement to Millhams Street, projecting the building line to the location of the north-west corner of the old hall and placing chalk marks based on J. E. Holloway's plan giving external dimensions of 20 feet by 46 feet 3 inches

Fig.15

This photograph is a group shot by the Mill Stream and the ruins of the Constable's House. Ex-Mayoral badges were worn. From Left to Right: Edward Coope, Michael Winfield, Michael Hodges, Mrs Norma Fox and David Fox.

In 1851, the members were very unhappy about the new pew arrangements for them at the Priory Church; yet their complaint to the Churchwardens was most elegantly expressed. Their 'attention was requested to the fact that the accommodation allotted to the Mayor and Burgesses in lieu of their former Seat in the Church is not so great either as that afforded by the old Corporation seat or as that which the Corporation was led to expect when first their consent was asked to the alterations in the Church and that the Churchwardens be requested to inform the Mayor and Burgesses what further accommodation they propose to afford them.' The purchase of cushions followed in the next year. In 1855, it was decided to ask the Churchwardens to restore the original Corporation Pew. Just a week later, the difficulty still seemed to be rankling as it was resolved that 'any future processions to the Church shall be in the discretion of the Mayor', who was George Ferrey. Matters were settled by July 1856 because a 'square pew plan', involving a space 11 feet by 9 feet 6 inches was found acceptable. The proposal by the new Mayor, William Ferrey, was duly seconded and resolved by the Corporation. An amendment by James Druitt, that the pew would be arranged so that members might sit facing each other, was not even seconded – perhaps there was already quite enough eye contact in the Council Chamber!

There were, as now, occasions of conflict and disagreement at the Town Hall. With the members often having major interests, it was inevitable quite apart from normal differences of opinion. In a probable case of conflict of interest on 17th May 1854, a Memorial to the Admiralty was being proposed by James Druitt. The voting was five for sending it and four against – it was therefore sent. One of those voting against was the boat-builder and father of thirteen, George Holloway. The purpose of the missive was to request the urgent attention of the Admiralty to the large coastal erosion caused by the profitable Hengistbury Mining Company, which was run by John Edward Holloway, a son of George. The majority of members could see the risk and wanted it stopped as soon as possible. The Company's removal of ironstones at the Head was indeed putting the town at long-term risk of flooding. Today, there is no disagreement amongst coastal engineers that the mining has left a disastrous legacy. Hence, despite the provision of considerable employment to the men of the town, the mining was even then most controversial. Indeed, some think it hastened the death of Sir George Rose, who watched in despair from his house at Sandhills as the headland disappeared.

In a possible sign of a heated argument, the Burgess George Holloway was the only member out of nine who did not sign the minute on

Fig.16

Watercolour of Castle Street c. 1830

(Reproduced by courtesy of the Red House Museum, Christchurch)

This picture was photographed by Mr. H.E. Miller, a verger at the Priory Church in Edwardian times. The watercolour itself was painted by an unknown artist from the side of Town Bridge away from town. However, the setting of the hall, as a terminating vista at the end of Castle Street, has been enhanced by showing the buildings on its south side rather further south.

17th May 1854. As they say, 'blood is thicker than water!' Sadly, he died in November of the same year at the age of 59. By September, Captain Vetch had reported to the Admiralty that the ironstone mining was a 'great evil' that should be stopped. Had his report been implemented, it would have taken away one of J. E. Holloway's business ventures. There must certainly have been some tension between him and the Council – at the same time that Druitt and Rose were trying to stop his mining enterprise, he was being asked by the Corporation to produce designs for the Town Hall.

In 1856, the Town Clerk was instructed to express the consent of the Corporation to the proposed railway. That year, there was ongoing consideration of the St. Mary Magdalen Hospital with a view to disposal of funds for the benefit of the poor, sick and infirm.

So much for the historical work of the Corporation before the 1860 rebuilding of the Town Hall. Even though these are just a small number of examples, perhaps enough has been said to show that there is little comparison with the present time. In essence, the members did important work but on a very small scale.

Returning to the unfortunate siting of the building where all such business was transacted, it is said that, even in the middle of the 19th century, the sheer weight of traffic justified its removal. At a key public meeting in 1857 to consider a rebuilding proposal, the Borough's M.P. referred to the 'inconvenient and dangerous site of the present building, which had been a matter of almost universal regret during the 67 years he had known the neighbourhood.' *Fig.15* is another picture painted it would appear from the house looking over Town Bridge along Castle Street. From this angle, it really appears that the hall is blocking the road fully or that there is some mistake by the artist. However, that part is correct due to the turning and widening of Castle Street just out of view.

There is no doubt that the position of the Third Town Hall was unsatisfactory in relation to the roads around it, as recognised locally for many years. Nonetheless, as the next chapter will explain, it was not the only pressure for relocation. Logically enough, such pressures meant that in terms of longevity, this was the least successful of all the town's halls.

CHAPTER FOUR

RESOLUTION: UPGRADE AS EXISTING

Despite the 'traffic-impeding' setting of the Third Town Hall, it was in regular use and could have so continued with the benefit of certain improvements. However, it was much too small for the needs of the 1850s. For example, comment was made in a letter published on 21st October 1865 concerning a dispute about unpaid subscriptions for the new building cost. In it, Town Clerk James Druitt mentioned that the Corporation had long felt that the previous building was 'wholly inadequate to the wants of the town'.

Yet another reason contributing to the move may possibly have been problems from certain people then known as 'roughs'. From 5th November 1850, many came into town night after night for over a month, indulging in rioting and putting the Town Hall at risk. On one occasion, a tar-filled barrel was lit on the ground level stones of the Market House, putting it in danger of being burnt down! Special constables were finally sworn in for three months from 10th December 1850. Certainly, all building options to solve the problem included no market area, which seemed to provide an attractive gathering place for the 'roughs'.

Having failed to agree terms to buy nearby property, the Corporation's next idea was to turn the ground level market area into floor space. At a stroke, it would have been possible to more than double the limited accommodation, but there was a serious disadvantage – it could not later be extended to one side without impinging on the highway. On the other hand, a much larger replacement site, whilst costly, would solve everything including the traffic problem, the inadequate accommodation and the need for flexibility to extend. In the event, as we have seen, the Council wisely opted for such relocation – indeed, the new structure, on part of the large open plot known as Blanchard's Yard in the High Street, was greatly enlarged to the rear as part of the building project.

The real start of the whole process was in March 1834 when George William Tapps was graciously thanked by the Corporation for his 'munificent offer of a piece of ground as a site whereon to rebuild the Town Hall'. The perceived difficulty at that time was a lack of funds and the possible need for an Act of Parliament to permit the removal of the Town Hall. As a result, a different solution was attempted. *Fig.17* shows the

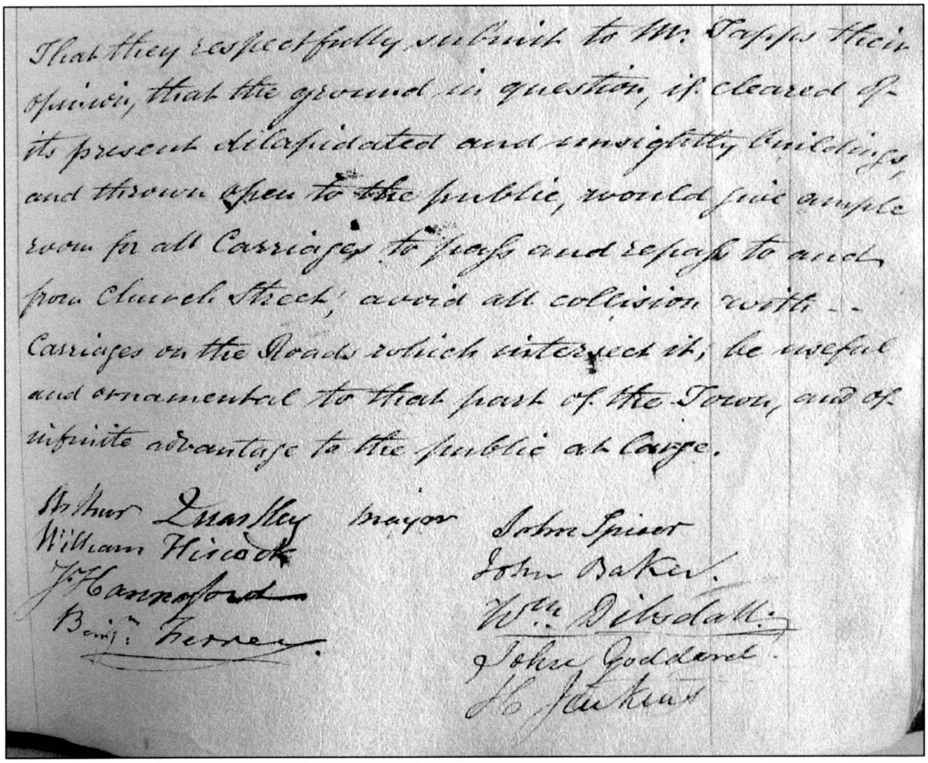

Fig.17

The Corporation's attempt to solve the traffic problem in 1834
(Reproduced by courtesy of Dorset History Centre Ref. DC/CC/Acc 7982 Box 9)

In this extract from the Old Minute Book dated 22 March 1834, it can be seen that a resolution was passed to try and persuade an adjoining landowner to help '...avoid all collisions with carriages on the road...' Mr. Tapps had kindly offered his land for a new hall, but it was not pursued due to concerns that it was beyond the legal powers of the Corporation to build one in this way. However, as a second best, the attempt was made by the Mayor Arthur Quartley and his Burgesses to secure it for reasons of traffic safety. Hence, even in 1834, a better hall was desired, as was a road improvement. Nothing came of this initiative.

Council's response, implying that the Tapps' land should be thrown into the public highway, thereby avoiding future collisions of carriages. Nothing was said about the payment of any consideration to the landowner for clearing the site and making it available for the purpose and nothing came of the idea. By May, it was felt necessary to seek counsel's opinion about the need for an Act to remove the hall, as financed by mortgaging Corporation property. In June, the opinion was received but not at all encouraging – the whole matter was postponed 'until the determination of governments relative to Corporations be made known'. One can sense some disappointment here as the whole idea went into abeyance.

Whilst the relocation need stayed unresolved, ordinary decisions still had to be taken. For instance, in 1847, it was resolved to sell the Winchester Measures and use the money for a register stove, fender and fire irons to be fitted in the hall. Presumably, there was insufficient use of these measuring aids for dry volume (bushels, pecks etc.) first devised in the 10th century, but a particular wish for the comfort of new gas heating in the Council Chamber. On 14th September 1850, an estimate (hand delivered that day) was accepted from Mr. Belbin for £3. 10s. to clean and repair the roof of the hall and take down and rebuild its chimney. The price does sound reasonable. Yet that same month, there was discussion about the propriety of taking steps to procure the old buildings at the corner of Church Street and Castle Street – the scheme to provide a new Town Hall was evidently still a live issue. Moreover, no more concerns arose then or later about the operation being 'beyond the powers' of the Corporation. A year later, a new specialist (E. Watts 'in room of' Richard Scott dec'd) was appointed to look after the Town Clock at a guinea a year. In January 1852, a new clock rope was receipted at 7s. 6d. (*Fig.18*). From Michaelmas that year, Cornhill was paid for another year's fire insurance based on a value of £450 and a premium of £1. 0s. 3d. Some wasted maintenance expenses must have been a little frustrating as money was then very tight and any new hall would clearly be very costly.

In September 1852, Admiral Walcott, the Borough's M.P., offered £200 towards the cost of a more commodious hall to be built and the old site to be 'thrown open'. He felt that this would be very good for the town. By September 1853, Sir George Gervis was apparently willing to consider any proposal for his land near to the hall. Authority was duly given to negotiate on behalf of the Corporation up to £80 purchase price, failing which a lease at a nominal figure was favoured. The following April, the Gervis land was to be bought if possible at up to £60. It is not clear why the limit reduced in this way over a few months. But the negotiations proved

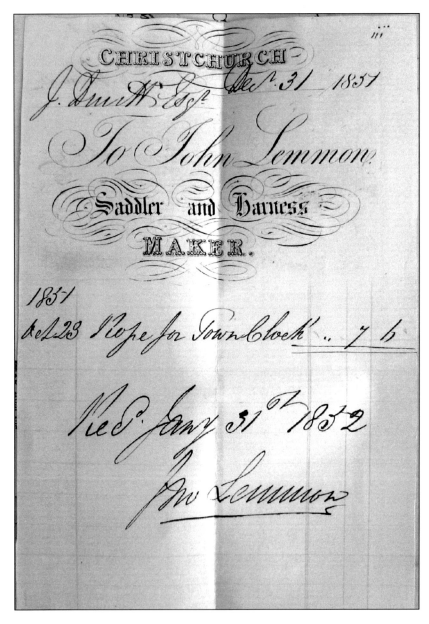

Fig.18

Rope for the Town Clock

(Reproduced by courtesy of Dorset History Centre Ref. DC/CC/Acc 7982 Box 9)

On New Year's Eve in 1851, John Lemmon provided this rope for the benefit of the clock that was never replaced in the new hall. For years, regular maintenance of this clock had been needed and perhaps it (or its cost) was not universally popular amongst the members of the Corporation. In March 1862, authority was given for it to be sold by the Mayor.

awkward with a June 1854 minute that there was no prospect of securing this land on any reasonable terms – necessary repairs were therefore put in hand.

Would the owner be prepared to lease the land for a public road? His suggestion in December of £4 per year (reduced from £5 earlier in the same month) on a 21-year lease was regarded by the Council as a major over-valuation and so declined. At this point, it was far from clear what might be the solution to the problems of traffic and cramped accommodation. Had those negotiations been carried on with the previous owner Tapps, who did not seem to want payment if his land was to be used for a new hall, the entire story could have been very different. So it is that such matters as rebuilding Town Halls can be determined by luck more than anything else!

On 19th March 1855, it was decided to proceed on the footing that the existing building would have to be retained – yet, within just two years, the opposite was true. On that day, there were the usual type of decisions, such as cleaning the Town Clock for 25 shillings and ordering a new Town Pump. However, it was also resolved that the Mayor was to create and put forward a plan for a Town Hall upgrade to a future Corporation meeting. In July, the architect, John Edward Holloway, was asked to produce conversion plans with an entrance and outside covered staircase at the west end of the south side. From *Fig.13*, it can be seen this section of Church Street would have been the quiet part and the extension not too intrusive. The next month, Admiral Walcott handed his cheque for £200 to the Mayor giving him free reign in how it might be used.

A meeting in early August 1855 looked at the scheme. The whole of the ground level was to be enclosed and made into two rooms. The ceiling of the first floor was to be raised if possible and the whole upper part to be thrown into one room. It was minuted that since the plan was not for the benefit of the Mayor and Burgesses but for the town, the Mayor was to call a meeting of the Inhabitants. It was hoped they would also contribute as the fear was that costs would be not less than £400. The Inhabitants met eight days later and the Council reconvened on 27th August 1855 with the benefit of the minutes of the Inhabitants' meeting – the Corporation had truly gone into overdrive! *The Christchurch Times and General Advertiser* of 1st September 1855 reported that the Inhabitants were 'agreeable to the alterations in the Town-hall buildings'.

Something had finally been decided. Or so it then seemed. The Holloway scheme provided an enclosed staircase at the eastern end of the existing building with a closet below it. The flooring of the ground level was to be in deal, a second fireplace was to be installed in the first floor, partitions were planned, rooms were to have wainscotting, a ventilator was to be made in the cupola and the first floor ceiling was finally resolved to be raised. These are clear intentions based on the formal wish to proceed with the conversion – they were not at the time a consideration of options. The architect was then required to produce plans and specifications for the annual meeting on 8th September 1855.

CHAPTER FIVE

U-TURN: WE MUST RELOCATE TO A BIG SITE

Now that it was all going to happen, a negative feeling surfaced. Do we really want to go through with this solution, or could we do better? When the architect's plans were produced for the meeting of 8th September 1855, the first signs of wavering can be detected: instead of approving them and putting them in hand, the matter was adjourned for further consideration six days later. In addition, the funding resolution used the words: 'if these plans are carried out'. Subject to that extremely important word 'if', the Corporation were to defray any costs beyond the £200 given by Admiral Walcott. By 14th September, one can see some sense of resignation at a necessary but not completely satisfactory scheme. The Mayor was instructed not to seek tenders from contractors until the following Friday in case he should 'receive information inducing him to call a meeting to consider any other scheme'. One could scarcely have a stronger indication of the members having second thoughts. Nonetheless, although it appears that something different was in the wind, it did not materialise because tenders were duly received and opened in October 1855, ranging from £390 to £498. It was decided to accept the lowest from Belbin and Stone.

John Edward Holloway was a most energetic man, who combined being an architect, Mayor of Christchurch on three occasions, coal merchant and proprietor of the Hengistbury Mining Company. Some idea can be gained of his sense of determination from *Fig.21*. No doubt his was not an easy life being one of thirteen siblings and he decided to make his mark as strongly as possible. *Fig.19* is a reproduction of his plan dated 1855 of the proposed ground floor. Apart from the staircase extension, this plan depicts almost exactly the same footprint as our present building, the 'Mayor's Parlour', fronting Saxon Square. In the normal convention of architectural drawings, he has shown the new work in a different colour, something which is not clear in the illustration. Suffice it to say that the ground level is shown as it would look converted to Council use (as one large room and one small room) from open-arched market use. Extra hearths and chimneys can be seen as can the enclosed and attractive curved staircase.

Fig.20 is derived from part of Holloway's upper floor plan. Evidently,

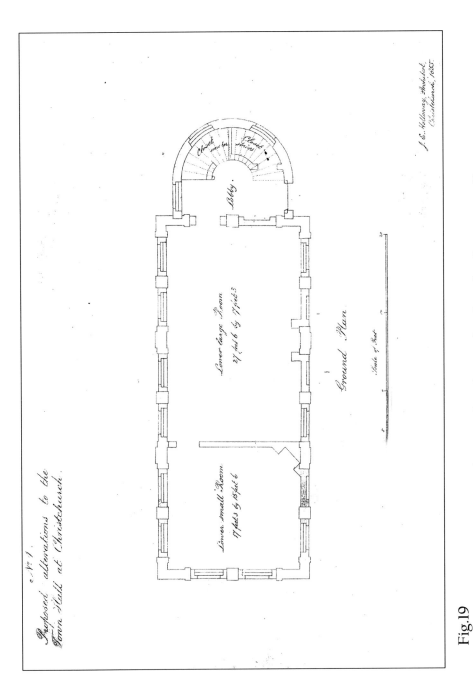

Fig.19

Upgrade plan dated 1855 for the Third Town Hall
(Reproduced by courtesy of Christchurch Local History Society)

J. E. Holloway produced this scheme to alter the hall and provide the Corporation with more space. Here we can see the ground level market area made into two rooms each with a fireplace and the curved side extension for an enclosed staircase. Since the existing hall was approached by stairs within the building plan, this was an opportunity to more than double the floor area of the Town Hall.

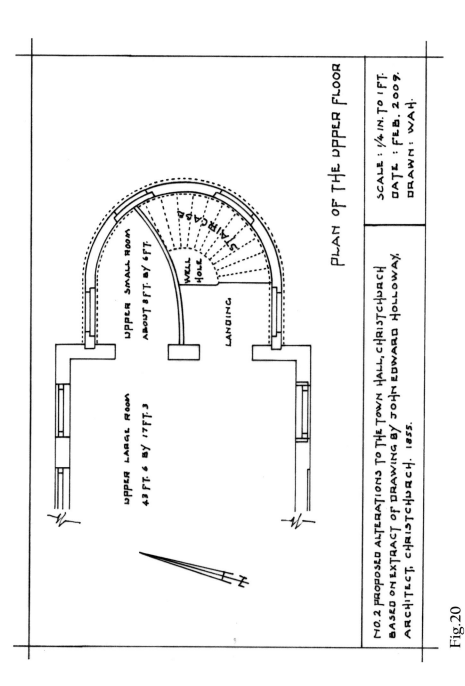

Fig. 20

Part of first floor upgrade plan dated 1855
(Based on drawing held by Christchurch Local History Society)

The author's sketch shows one end of the Holloway scheme at the upper level. It would have been a very big improvement to the existing facility. After a tender had been accepted, it was decided to relocate the Town Hall instead and these upgrade works were cancelled. Compensation for loss amounting to £20 had to be paid to the successful would-be contractor.

the idea was fully to make over the lower level to Council use together with two closets and provide a small extra room on the first floor. Although there is no North Point on the original plan, one has been shown here based on what was said in Council Minutes. His preference, to put the staircase at the eastern end of the Third Town Hall, was wiser than the previous suggestion from the members that it be tacked on to the south side. Since we know that there was no sign of any external staircase on pictures from the time (*Fig.10* and *Fig.12*), it follows that there would have been a staircase within the 1746 structure from market level to the first floor. Hence, Holloway's upgrade scheme would have more than doubled the enclosed floor area available to the Council.

Matters again seemed fairly 'cut and dried'. Despite the wavering, nothing better had turned up and a tender for the conversion and upgrade had been accepted. The scheme was certainly relatively inexpensive. Yet eventually, Christchurch opted to relocate. The reason for the U-turn was Admiral Walcott's opinion reported at a very late stage to a meeting on 1st November 1855. He felt that spending such a large sum on the existing Town Hall was 'injudicious' and offered to increase his own contribution from £200 to £300 'if it be removed'. With the Corporation's obvious reservations about the conversion scheme, he was certainly pushing at an open door. Despite his extra money being a small proportion of the much greater cost of a removal plan, such a solution was now vigorously pursued by resolutions. A subcommittee was immediately formed to report back on the feasibility of rebuilding on the Council-owned land by Little Bridge. The nature of any such new building was to be considered and there would need to be more consultation with the Inhabitants. It was also recognised that some payoff would be needed to those whose tender had been accepted. In view of his key contribution to the relocation, some brief biographical notes about Admiral Walcott now follow:

> The Admiral was apparently the main trigger for the decision of Christchurch Corporation in 1855 to relocate the Town Hall. Despite the fact that a scheme to alter the existing Town Hall had just been approved by the members, he wanted a new building altogether. The U-turn happened in the month following the acceptance of a tender for the alterations works. Although we know that there was some reluctance by the members to convert the existing Town Hall, that was indeed the approved resolution of the day – Walcott's opinion and offer of a larger donation caused the resolution to be 'unscrambled' and compensation for loss was later paid to the winning tenderers, Belbin and Stone. What sort of man was this, who had the ability and foresight to press so strongly and successfully for the relocation option?

Having joined the Navy in 1802 as a midshipman at the age of 12, Walcott steadily rose through the ranks, aided by some excellent reports from superior officers. For instance, he played a valiant part in three ship captures, so resulting in a letter to the Controller of the Navy from Rear Admiral Sir Samuel Hood in 1808: 'A more deserving good young officer does not exist.' This was high praise indeed.

By 1814, Hood was suggesting Flag Lieutenant Walcott be promoted to Commander, referring to 'situations he has filled with much capacity and judgement.' But unfortunately, with the naval cutback following Napoleon's defeat at Waterloo in 1815, his active service was delayed for years due to a dying wish of Hood. Sir Samuel wanted Walcott to report on recent operations to the Admiralty, because he was the best person to carry out such an important task. Biographical records held at the Red House Museum indicate that by doing so, he was away for too long and lost the chance to be Post Captain by 1816 in India. Finally, in 1822, he was posted to Jamaica Station. It involved initially convoy protection and later, a search around eastern Cuba, for the pirates who were disrupting British trade. It was his finest hour – a pirate crew of about 75 European Spaniards were certainly disrupted by Walcott!

In a most gallant endeavour as Captain of the Tyne, he reportedly took small boats into the line of heavy fire and boarded the schooner Zaragozana creating such panic that nearly all the pirate crew threw themselves into the sea. Some ten were killed, 15 wounded and 28 captured, with others believed drowned. Later, 16 escapees were captured. Royal Naval losses were much less – two killed and five wounded. Many, including the pirate leader, were duly hanged. It was to be the last naval action of the future Member of Parliament of Christchurch.

Years later as Admiral Walcott, his retirement was that of a country gentleman at the family home of Winkton Lodge – a large house and grounds of 24 acres, until recently occupied by Homefield School. His later years may have been idyllic amongst the trees, lawns, barns and cottages on this vast site close to the River Avon. The son of an Army Officer, Walcott had even married a daughter, Charlotte, of a Lieutenant Colonel of the Bengal Artillery. A family tree exists showing three of his four brothers were in the Services and he had four sisters besides. It was a very military family that is rather hard to imagine in our time – at least until the next generation, where John and Charlotte had three daughters and a son, who became an eminent ecclesiastic and writer.

When he was M.P. for Christchurch from 1852 until his death, Admiral Walcott was certainly very generous to the town, giving Christmas money for the Mayor to spend on blankets for the poor and a beef and plum pudding dinner for the inmates of the Workhouse. His grounds were made available for fetes, concerts and anniversary teas to celebrate Coronation Day. He gave prizes to the Agricultural Society and was a frequent honoured guest at various dinners, replying for example to toasts on behalf of the Army and Navy. He was a generous donor also to the Priory Church and St. James's Church, Pokesdown, where his wife was buried in 1863. He was buried in the same large table tomb, in 1868, which remains to this day just to the south-east of the Chancel. Apart from being a staunch Conservative in Parliament, he was also a Justice of the Peace and Deputy Lieutenant for Hampshire.

Some three years after his death, the Admiral's daughter, Miss Constance Walcott, presented Lewis Holloway's amazing portrait to the town. Lewis was a brother of the Holloway (another John Edward) that produced the plans for the Corporation, firstly to convert and then to rebuild the Town Hall. Apart from his obvious talent as an artist, painting this amazing portrait at the age of 20, Lewis is also notable for his tragic early death at just 24 years old. The date of the portrait, 1857, is also the date that the site for the new Town Hall was acquired. The family's gift to Christchurch Borough was officially recognised by a resolution of thanks dated 30 May 1871.

It is safe to say that Admiral Walcott was a man of considerable courage, judgement and commitment to the town and one who correctly saw that it would be far better to relocate the Town Hall than to alter it.

Once more however, progress was by 'fits and starts'. It was not until July 1856 that another real step was taken – to adjourn for 15 days and that members 'do endeavour to obtain further information respecting the sites which have been mentioned or any others that may be suggested.' At a later meeting that month, there was a resolution for the Mayor to 'call a meeting of the Corporation and Town Committees to confer upon the subject of the removal of the Town Hall.' On 30th August 1856, the *Christchurch Times* reported in detail about the deliberations of the Inhabitants Committee. An offer had been made (for nominal consideration) of waste land owned by Sir George Gervis, near to the Third Town Hall. Almost certainly, this is the site originally offered by Tapps in 1834 and later described as having buildings in poor condition. It was now described as 'vacant and disfigured', and a 'disfigurement and eyesore'. Plans were produced by 'our young townsman Lewis Holloway' for a Reading Room, a large room for public purposes and a room for the use of the Corporation. This could have been added to a house site, where the house would have been bought from a Mr. Pack. It is not now clear exactly how such a redevelopment would have looked but it would still have been a much more restricted site than the one eventually chosen in the High Street.

Fig.21

John Edward Holloway (1821-1901)

Holloway was a man of many parts – coal merchant, architect, Corporation member, three times Mayor, at one time Chairman of the Board of Guardians of the Christchurch Workhouse and proprietor of the Hengistbury Mining Company. His work on the Town Hall upgrade is most evident in the series of his drawings now held in the History Room of the Christchurch Local History Society. He was regularly asked to produce fresh plans as the job progressed. As a coal merchant, he supplied the town's quay where a large coal store was kept for many years. His barges then returned to Southampton ballasted with the ironstones mined from the headland. From there, they were shipped to South Wales furnaces to create iron – altogether a most profitable though controversial undertaking. Essentially a keen businessman, Holloway must have been most put out by the various attempts to stop the mining and preserve the town against the sea. His father, boat builder and Burgess George Holloway, voted (unsuccessfully) against the plan for the Corporation to put its weight behind the 'stop mining' campaign – today, as a councillor, he would have had to declare an interest and decline to vote.

Fig.22

James Druitt (1816-1904)
(Reproduced by courtesy of the Red House Museum, Christchurch)

Druitt was certainly one of those unusual people who 'made things happen' in 19th century Christchurch. His influence as Town Clerk and Corporation member over many years was strongly exercised in conjunction with his skills as a solicitor and property dealer. These abilities greatly helped the relocation project with important matters such as regularising the site boundaries. He was well able to take a hard line when he felt it appropriate and would 'stick to his guns' when required. For instance, he could see better than many the need for the town to own and control the new Town Hall and also the need to oppose the disastrous ironstone mining at Hengistbury Head. Another major legacy for the town derives from the site assembly efforts of him and his family resulting in the present-day Druitt Library and Gardens.

When the Inhabitants Committee went on to debate the option of a removal to a site in the High Street, there was a strong majority by vote for that solution. It was pointed out that such a site would allow a much better building with scope for extending and having space all around it. There would be air and light on every side and views of the surrounding country, whilst the cost might not be any greater. The report confirmed the concurrence of benefactor Admiral Walcott and indeed indicated he had thought of the site as the best one in the town for the purpose. The front part of the plot owned by Sir George Pocock was stated to be obtainable 'at a comparatively modest price'. It was of course Blanchard's Yard. Thanks were to be given to Gervis and the hope expressed that his land could still be bought by the Corporation and 'no doubt rounded and railed off and something planted or erected'. In this connection, it is interesting that *Fig.23* does show land at the corner of Church Street and Castle Street as railed off in a fashion consistent with that expressed hope.

This was the essential breakthrough. As explained to the Corporation meeting of 8th September 1856, 'Sir G. Pocock was willing to part with land called Blanchard's Yard on terms on which the site for the Town Hall would cost about £250.' It almost goes without saying that there must have been discussions with him behind the scenes for all this to be known. There was no prevarication – Druitt was instructed 'to obtain the site accordingly.' This he did by the next year, personally buying the entirety of Blanchard's yard with a view to reselling part to the Corporation.

Thus, within two years of Holloway's drawings and specifications in 1855 to alter the existing premises, a public subscription was running for a rebuild on a different site. By 1860, the Fourth Town Hall was indeed finished and ready for public use. However, we shall see from the following chapter that the next stages were no easier than the decision about whether to convert or rebuild. The Corporation having chosen the more expensive solution, it all had to be organised, financed and implemented.

Fig.23

View across the High Street c.1865
after demolition of the Third Town Hall
(Reproduced by courtesy of the Red House Museum, Christchurch)

The hall was down by May 1859, so allowing the street corner to be 'opened up' for easier traffic. In this extremely early photograph, the Town Pump looms large in the foreground. It slightly obscures a building on the corner of High Street and Castle Street. That is still there, now occupied by O2, a mobile phone company, but the site of the hall was simply part of the road by 1865. Behind the railing fence may be some rubble, perhaps from the hall or from removal of the structure referred to as in poor condition in 1834 on the Tapps land. That corner site was redeveloped and is now occupied by fashion house Roberta (*Fig.14*).

CHAPTER SIX

PLANNING THE FOURTH HALL

Having determined in November 1855 to remove the Third Town Hall, instead of converting it, the Corporation was finally able in September 1857 to deposit an important document in the Town Chest – the conveyance for the new site at Blanchard's Yard in the High Street. But this was to be no ordinary replacement where the building was finished and then the occupier moved from old to new – here, the Council's normal work had to be carried out elsewhere in the town, whilst the stones of the Town Hall were recovered for re-use on the new site.

Drawings from the time make clear that the Council were sensibly considering their options. One was to have a new building three feet more in front-to-rear depth, 'than the present Town Hall' giving an internal measurement of 20 feet instead of 17 feet. This layout showed a police constable's house, a police sergeant's house with central yard and cells, all adjacent to the north-west side of a Town Hall rear extension measuring internally 64 feet by 30 feet. (Including a corridor, the length would have been 70 feet.) Although not built in this fashion, the scheme still demonstrated a wish to have a large extension to a front building that itself was virtually identical to the Third Town Hall. It also showed a perceived need for more policing around a new hall, harking back to the 1850 riots at the existing one. A further unrealised plan was to have the stairs in the middle of the proposed replacement building, rather than at one end, as finally constructed.

These examples, of an early intention to expand on the large replacement site, are more proof that traffic congestion was not the sole consideration driving the move – the Corporation wanted to see an upgrade. A working drawing even exists of a yet more costly choice with the new building's front elevation having eight arches instead of the six used for both the 1746 and the 1860 buildings actually erected. However, one of this plan's design changes, from the Third Town Hall, was adopted – a balustrade along the eaves. It is likely that there was adverse comment about such an embellishment at the time, especially considering the lack of a bell and clock in the new hall. A first floor balcony was also incorporated from this design.

It was however another drawing which was eventually adopted by

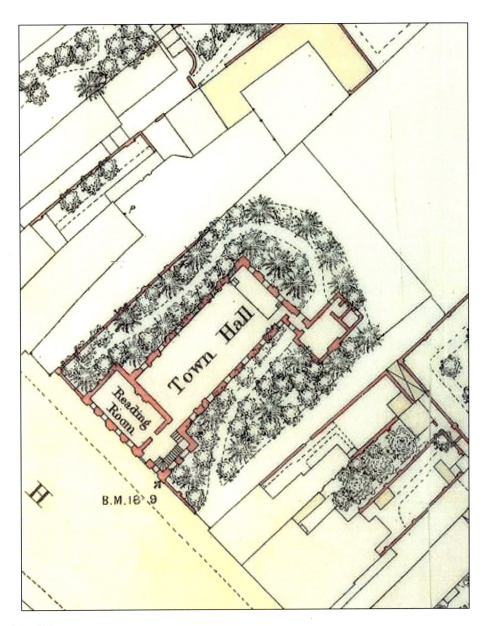

Fig.24

Fourth Town Hall in 1870
(Reproduced from the Ordnance Survey map of that date.
© Crown Copyright. 1/500 scale before enlargement)

By 1860, the front building, a close replica of the Third Town Hall, had been erected together with the main rear rectangular hall. The addition to that hall was a retiring room or ante room and 'tacked on' within a few years. Clearly, that completed the functionality of the main hall as it gave some accommodation for those due to appear on the stage.

the Council. This time, J. E. Holloway showed the Fourth Town Hall with a ground level Corporation Room of 29 feet by 17 feet internal dimensions and a first floor Reading Room of the same size. The ground level hall and staircase (13 feet by 17 feet) had a rear door opening to a simple large room marked Town Hall of 70 feet by 30 feet (again internally), shown with two hearths and chimneys along each side. In the event, the large rectangular extension, built to the rear of the Town Hall, was different from all these drawings having internal dimensions of about 27 feet by 63 feet. So much can be estimated partly from the large scale 1870 Ordnance Survey map (*Fig.24*), but mainly from scale drawings of later extension works. Moreover, instead of Holloway's central window in the main front elevation at the first floor, an elaborate balcony was provided.

    The difference, between approved plans and the smaller building erected, was mirrored in the Corporation decisions of the time. It was resolved to 'carry out the plans so far as the funds raised would enable it to be done.' The idea was to establish at a future public meeting how far the plans could be implemented with the funds raised by that time. In reality, this meant that the front two storey building would certainly be erected and the rear single storey hall extension would be made as large as funds allowed. In the meantime, the *Christchurch Times* strongly suggested that all should contribute to the costs.

    It is worth looking at a comparison of size between the two actual buildings, disregarding for now the rear hall. Using Holloway's alterations plan, the 1746 one scales at 20 feet by 46 feet 3 inches external. In contrast, my current measurements with a surveyor's tape for the 1860 one, now the 'Mayor's Parlour', are 20 feet by 46 feet 9 inches external – a virtually identical reinstatement, size for size. Thus far, it is clear that the town decided to have the best option of rebuilding a much improved facility for Christchurch on a very large green-field site. Various schemes were proposed and discussed leading eventually to the structure shown on the Ordnance Survey extract in *Fig.24*.

    Turning to an incidental story, there is some mystery concerning the Town Hall bell. It was reported in June 1951 that pieces of the bell, cast in 1737 and hung from the bell tower of the Third Hall, were found in a sack under the stage of the Fourth Hall. The finder was Christchurch Macebearer, Albert Cox. Since it was made well before the erection of the Third Hall, it may even have been in use for the ancient Tolsey. Certainly, the 1747 accounts for the erection of the Third Hall refer to the cost of a spring for the market bell.

    It was thought that the bell had been stolen, by a workman to sell as scrap, around the time of the relocation in 1859/1860 – instead, it had evidently been mislaid under the stage of the new hall, where it remained unseen until 1951! However, according to Dalton's *Bells and Belfries of Dorset* (published in 2000), a broken bell dated 1737, almost certainly by Tosier (or an associate) of Salisbury, had been stuck together and was residing in St. Michel's Loft Museum at the Priory Church. The 17 inch diameter bell is indeed still there with a description saying that the place in which it was hung is unknown. The date of 1737 is shown in figures ⅝ of an inch high. Dalton established that the 1737 bell (as stuck together) was indeed at the Red House until at least 12th July 1991 before going to the Priory Church.

In 1951, the Curator of the Red House Museum, Mr. Lavender, was reported as believing that another bell was procured for the Fourth Hall. This second bell, dated 1817, was found at some stage in the home of the Druitt family at 14-15 High Street. The maker was James Wells (casting from 1790 to 1825), from the Aldbourne foundry in Wiltshire. Both bells initially went to the Red House Museum. At the time, the idea was to exhibit the broken one and use the later one as a museum closing-time warning. Dalton was informed that the Wells bell was later transferred to another Hampshire museum. It must be fair comment to say that the current church exhibit is extremely likely to be the bell, which saw duty for the entire life of the Third Town Hall. Corporation minutes record that on 29th March 1862, it was resolved that the Mayor sell the old town clock, bell and weights – perhaps soon after the new hall was built, it was decided that a market bell was not needed and it was simply sold to James Druitt.

The Surveyor of Ways agreed to the purchase of the old site for the highway authority at £55, so providing today's improved road junction. If you take the land area as about 0.02 acres, which is derived from the footprint of the replacement building still standing, the cost represents about £2,750 per acre. Since we know that the purchase price of the 0.5 acres new site was £221, it follows that its value was deemed to be £442 per acre although nearly half of the total site was retained for future expansion. To be clear, the Corporation not only secured land and curtilage for an identical replacement, it also obtained enough land to erect a large new hall, and yet more land to the rear that could be built upon in the future. It really was a far-sighted acquisition. If these land prices sound a bit low even allowing for inflation, perhaps it will help to compare it to the land on Bournemouth's East Cliff going for about £5 per acre under the 1802 Inclosure Act! The Council's unused rear land was let in June 1860 to Mr. Butler for 30 shillings per annum.

If a highway authority were to instigate such an acquisition now, the compensation basis would almost certainly be a Rule Five Case, i.e. 'equivalent reinstatement' applicable where there is no general demand for that type of property. The word 'almost' applies because the Lands Tribunal does have discretion where the cost of equivalent reinstatement is enormously out of proportion to the property value. However, that would be unlikely to apply here. The claimant (the Council) would have to show to the acquiring authority (another Council) a bona fide intent to reinstate (easily shown) and be paid out on the basis of costs incurred (land purchase cost and building cost), so completely avoiding public subscriptions or donations. It is an example of how payments for public works can change from patronage and subscription in the former low-tax era to government-financed spending in our own high-tax but admittedly, more prosperous time. Yet perhaps even this remark needs some qualification in view of the very heated debate of 1865, outlined in the next chapter, about the alleged misuse of the subscription money.

To all the people claiming a permanent lack of efficiency and competence on the part of the Borough, it might be said that in truth, the relocation was a major success for the long-term benefit of Christchurch. Furthermore, it was one which should not be derided as a matter of luck, because the key decision in August 1856 was based, as we have seen, on the correctly perceived merit of a particular large site.

Over the years, considerable extensions became possible until the need for really major Council accommodation and for more town centre shops justified the Saxon Square scheme. Time proved that even this was a most appropriate town improvement. The shopping area east of the bypass was enlarged and focussed to the town's needs and the Civic Offices were purpose-built to full modern requirements on an ideal site towards the edge of the town centre. *Fig.25* indicates the prime position of Sir George Pocock's land as part of Christchurch before the site assembly needed for Saxon Square, but after the erection of the supermarket now occupied by Somerfield. Perhaps this illustration shows better than anything else the site's long-term importance and the wisdom of the Corporation in 'snapping it up' in 1857.

Fig.25

Setting of the Fourth Town Hall in 1974

(Aerial photograph by Allen White. Reproduced by courtesy of the Red House Museum and Christchurch Local History Society who jointly hold the copyright.)

What a change to Christchurch since the replacement site was purchased! That 1857 land is shown on the photograph, edged in a broken heavy line.

CHAPTER SEVEN

FRAUGHT BUT IN THE END TRIUMPHANT

We have reached the point where the final decision had been made to relocate and all the details had to be addressed. The process itself was not particularly smooth, accompanied as it was by financial worries, some local apathy and adverse comment. On the other side of the coin, there was enough generosity, vision and determination to see it though and win the day. Is it not strange how nothing seems to have changed despite our current modernity?

The best place to start looking at the chain of events may be the initial gift to the town, because it was this which enabled the whole thing to go ahead. In February 1857, Admiral Walcott's donation of £200 plus bank interest was placed in a special account to allow James Druitt, as Town Clerk, to proceed with the purchase of the land. The Corporation's first instalment of £50 was added to the same account. Holloway was now paid £6. 6s. for his work on the old conversion plans and asked to produce fresh ones for the new site. The same month, the extra £100 promised by Walcott was received and another £100 from his sister, Mrs. Dixon. On 16th February 1857, the site cost, including interest and legal expenses was standing at £227. 5s. 4d. including £221 being the price of the land. Conveyancing documentation eventually followed on 19th May 1857.

The 1843 Tithe Map extract at *Fig.1* shows Blanchard's Yard marked as Tithe Map Reference 4008 and the only large High Street plot without buildings down to the Mill Stream. The occupier at the time of the Tithe Book (marked as 1844) was George Gubbins. Between then and the 1870 date of the Ordnance Survey map (*Fig.24*), there was some boundary straightening to provide a more regularly shaped area of land. James Druitt owned land on both sides.

Druitt was indeed a main force in Christchurch for much of the 19th century holding the office of Town Clerk for some years and being elected Mayor five times. He was also noted for successful property dealing – the site for the Fourth Town Hall is an example. *Fig.22* shows him in his later years as a man of character and force. Yet in reminiscences dictated to his daughter, Barbara in 1888 at the age of 72, the impression is of considerable charm and indeed some diffidence. For example, at an early stage he remarks: 'It seems to me however to be rather a cheeky and also rather a difficult thing to plunge into autobiography when one has so little to say...'

The background is that John Coventry left Blanchard's Yard to his niece Augusta in a will of 1827; she later inherited it and married George Edward Pocock. They both (together with her son) sold it to James Druitt. The completion was 4th March 1857 and the price £300, including also adjoining land Tithe Map Reference 4007. Given a total land area of 1 acre 1 rood and 32 perches (1.45 acres), and the resale by him of part to the Corporation of precisely 0.5 acres at £221, it sounds like a very satisfactory deal for him. He secured thereby 0.95 acres for £79 only, although admittedly it was back land. There is no doubt that this method was an administrative convenience for both him and the Corporation – he purchased it with a view to reselling the front part.

Detailed resolutions were placed in the minutes. The land size was to be 90 feet by a depth of 244 feet, being the front part of 'Blanchard's Garden'. Perhaps the name was changed from Yard to Garden in order to sound better! Certainly, the plot length was reduced by two feet to 242 feet only in the conveyance plan. Incidentally, if you proceed that distance back from the High Street today, you reach the vehicular entrance to the upper level of the car park behind Somerfield Supermarket. This large area was in stark contrast to the site of the Third Town Hall amounting to 0.02 acres. Arrangements were identified for deducting the value of the back land at £80 per acre, for calculating certain frontage land deductions and reserving a ten-foot wide right of way to the retained land at the rear. The site was marked out and various boundary obligations were fixed as a matter of good conveyancing practice. Druitt owned land to the rear and on both sides of the rectangular site.

During the legal formalities, it was realised that there was a possible conflict of interest. As the purchaser's solicitor acting for the Corporation, could James Druitt act fairly when he was also the vendor? The boundary marking had already been done on the basis that he represented himself and the Council was represented by the Mayor and two other members. The solution was to consult prominent local solicitor Mr. Sharp, whose letter was read out to the meeting on 19th May 1857 – he was satisfied as to the sufficiency of the proposed conveyance document. It was duly signed by the Mayor Edward S. Elliott that very day and deposited in the Town Hall. Some of the back land down to the Mill Stream amounting to 2 roods and 8 perches (0.55 acres) was eventually acquired by the Council. It was sold by the Druitt family in 1922 for £190 as one lot in a sale.

In confirmation, by their edition of 30th May 1857, the *Christchurch Times* was able to announce the successful purchase by the Corporation of the new site opposite the National School Rooms and 'usually occupied by travelling circuses for the exhibition of horsemanship.' People must have felt that the Town Hall was simply being moved physically along the High Street. The stones certainly were so moved! The Committee met several times during one week deciding on a plan and on opening a Subscription List immediately. It was a time of some excitement amongst town leaders. Unfortunately, on 4th September 1857, an important public meeting in the Town Hall to receive the Committee report was poorly attended. It is clear from the tone of the comment in the *Christchurch Times* that the editor was somewhat exasperated generally about apathetic local attitudes to the relocation. He was right to be concerned. Four days later, a net credit balance was showing of only £330. 15s. 9d. This was the money in the bank after receiving donations with some bank interest on the one hand, and buying the land and paying incidental costs on the other. A start had been made, but there was nothing like enough cash yet available to build the hall.

Operating on a slightly different wavelength, or with different information from the town records, the *Christchurch Times* 'talked up' the receipts. In September 1857, it was reported that nearly £1,000 (correct figure about £564) had been collected by subscription, apart from many other promises of help without sums specified. A Subscription List was to be published no doubt to encourage any backsliders! As touched upon in the next chapter, the paper certainly believed in piling on and maintaining the moral pressure. For instance, less than two months before the start of the building works, the editorial of 19 March 1859 encouraged former complainants to 'examine their bank-book, their cash box, their purse, or it may be their old stocking, and give liberally as their means will allow them.' Moreover, the spectre was raised of future generations being able to say: 'our fathers were niggardly.'

Perhaps with this sort of sentiment in mind, in a letter of 12th January 1858, Charlotte Walcott had written to the paper: 'May I beg you to be so obliging as to add my name to the List of Subscribers for the Erection of a new Town Hall at Christchurch for the sum of One Hundred Pounds, it being my wish thus to testify the sincere interest I take in any undertaking which is likely to promote or increase the prosperity and well-being of a neighbourhood in which I dwell, and to which with Admiral Walcott, and each member of my family, I feel bound by the kindly ties of sympathy and regard.' It was probably no accident that immediately next to this entry in the paper by Mrs. Walcott, was one extolling the generous gift by her husband – each year he made a seasonable gift of £40 for coals to be given away amongst the poor.

The credit and debit ledger for the new Town Hall fund throws light on other matters. From it, we can see that the Town Clerk Mr. Druitt paid £3 per year rental for the land pending its development. His temporary use of the land, at that time still a meadow, is likely to have been for pasture. As for donations, the M.P.'s family was extremely generous supplying between them £600 and the Earl of Malmesbury donated another £100. Otherwise, the Council made regular payments of £50 when able and others were more limited with donations varying from five shillings to £25. Fire insurance was debited at more than three times the cost attaching to the old hall. It can also be seen that there was a need for considerable and expensive shrub clearance on the new site. Once built, contributions to the fund resulted from events held.

By February 1859, the Plan had been decided on and tenders from builders were now to be sought. Next month, the documents for removal and enlargement were ready for contractors to inspect and then provide estimates. Tenders were £1,552. 13s.; £1,075; £1,353; £1,390 and £1,370 – the lowest from Mr. Wickham of Poole was accepted subject to the Corporation being satisfied about him. It was reported on 30 April 1859 that removal works were to begin on 2 May 1859. 'More daylight will be let into the neighbouring houses, and we shall have a fine open space...' To ensure that there was no complacency amongst prospective donors, the *Christchurch Times* stressed that there were other costs, including land price, fittings and supervision of works. In addition – 'it has now been determined in order at once to make the large Hall as convenient and complete as possible, to extend the length as much as will be compatible with the general proportions of the building.' In other words, by April 1859, the nominated contractor had been signed up to build a front building, which would be virtually identical to the 1746 Third Town Hall, but also have a large rear hall of initially uncertain size.

Despite this being an unusual arrangement, it all worked out in the end. No doubt there was give and take with the Clerk of Works, Mr. Davis, acting as a sort of honest broker in adjusting the stage payments and final total due from the Corporation to Mr. Wickham as required. In most building jobs, the specification changes during the process to reflect the changing needs of the building owner. In this case, the rear hall was somewhat smaller than planned but the front building was embellished with balcony and balustrade. There was never any question of having more than a very small short-term debt. In all, six stage payments were made to the builder for the final scheme, as altered, at a total cost of £1,145. 16s. 11d. incidentals such as the Clerk's wages, insurance, bank interest, gravel, shrub clearance, planting, legal costs and advertising were relatively minor. It was a well-managed building project, resulting in the town securing a freehold interest in a much better Town Hall – and free of all debt before the end of 1861.

Financing, however, was somewhat precarious. There were no government grants or other subsidies to be had in those days. The Borough's property and income were strictly limited as shown by a minute in March 1841 giving total annual income of only £67. 7s. The early promise of £300 from the Admiral, as the biggest donor, was most welcome. Indeed, his final total was £400. Nonetheless, it compared to a land price of more than £200 and to the eventual building tenders, the lowest at £1,075 plus extra costs. In the whole of 1858, only about £101 was added to the credit side of the ledger. In the end, the stage was reached where a decision had to be made. Yet it is clear that at the time the go-ahead was given to the successful contractor in April 1859, money was still insufficient. In round figures, £927 had then been raised. Of this sum, £234 had been spent already and much of the project's cost still had to be found. The figures just did not add up and there may have been a slightly desperate note to the next stage of fund-raising.

As the old hall was being put into builder's hands for demolition and salvage, the work of the Corporation had to be continued elsewhere. In April 1859, James Druitt's office, within what is now the present Christchurch Library, became the Town Hall for the duration. Some of the old furniture was made available to the Court House and the use of the Justices and the surplus sold. At this point, a claim was put in by one of the successful tenderers for the 1855 conversion scheme. The Council felt that no real loss had been sustained but agreed that up to £20 could be paid if appropriate and this amount is found to have been the settlement to Stone and Belbin in August 1859.

By its issue of 14th May 1859, the paper reported that 'the old Hall is down.' *Fig.23* is a photograph giving no hint of the Third Town Hall – by that time its former site was merely part of the road. The area behind a post and rail timber fence still has rubble remaining very possibly from its demolition. However, that area was later redeveloped and occupied by boot makers Froud Bros. – today the ground floor is fashion house Roberta. The Committee had been evenly split, four each way, on whether to set the new building back 25 feet to allow a carriage drive, or have it in line with the other houses – the casting vote of Chairman J. K. Welch decided the matter in favour of not setting it back.

The large rectangular single-storey extension, in contemplation

Fig.26 Edward VII Coronation Parade in Christchurch High Street, August 1902
(Reproduced by courtesy of the Red House Museum, Christchurch)

In this marvellous photograph by Alfred Mallett, the Town Hall can be seen as almost contributing to the event and festivities – a day of flags and displays. Little did anyone know about the forthcoming tragedy of two World Wars.

from the earliest stage, was erected at the same time as the front building. It can be seen on the O.S. map in *Fig.24*, together with an extra side extension. According to ex-Mayor William Tucker in his *Reminiscences* of 1920, the old stone was salvaged and, redressed as required. Specialist but informal comment has kindly been supplied by Dorchester architect, Anthony Jaggard, about some differences between the 1746 hall and the front part of the 1860 one. He feels that the hand-made red stocks of what is now the 'Mayor's Parlour' do not have the appearance of reclaimed bricks. That would have been a labour-intensive task at a time when new bricks were freely available and not expensive. Besides, many more were needed anyway in order to build the rear hall. However, he agrees that stones would certainly have been redressed in this sort of case and indeed many more required to provide the balustrade and balcony. It is also interesting that there has been some remodelling e.g. the keystones, to the arches above the ground level, are somewhat deeper in the latest hall implying a slightly higher first floor level. In summary, the replacement was extremely similar but not identical to the original.

With expenditure running ahead of income, there was a period of deficit as financed by the Wilts and Dorset Bank (now Lloyds Bank), whose premises were opposite the Third Town Hall. On 11th June 1861, bank interest was charged at only £5. 14s. 4d., a figure much outweighed by the bank's earlier £20 donation to the removal fund. By July 1860, the bank's help was certainly needed with the cumulative costs then being about £1,483 compared to donations etc. at about £1,351. At least the work had then been completed – the last payment to the builder was made that month and in August the Corporation resolved that the hall was freely available for approved public uses such as for a Reading Room.

However, well before this resolution, some remunerative use was made of the new building with the earliest ledger record of the 'room' being for W. Greenhead on 8th and 9th May 1860. The total payment for both occasions was one guinea plus ten shillings for gas. On 15th May, Mr. Harding gave a lecture on the Great Social Evil in the 'hall' at the same cost except the price of gas was five shillings only. The *Christchurch Times* commented that the new Town Hall was well suited for public meetings, being 'a noble building for such a town as ours.' Even the quiet-spoken were heard distinctly through the whole room. Some 450 attended and space was left for 50 to 100 more. Over time, the hall moved out of debt and provided a fine new amenity for the town. It was indeed a triumph.

An appreciation of the success of the scheme can be gleaned from a close look at *Fig. 26*, a photograph taken of the High Street at the time of the celebration of the coronation of King Edward VII. The Town Hall lends civic presence to the whole street scene – although only about a century ago, it was a totally different era. It was the time of Empire, high confidence in the nation and simple patriotic fervour. Many, perhaps the majority, 'dressed to their class' and 'knew their place'. The unprecedented horror of World War I was unknown, as were the material benefits that we take for granted today. The Fourth Town Hall fitted in very much better than the previous one would have done, at this, the start of the Edwardian Era.

Meanwhile, the newspaper correctly reported receipts by August 1860 of about £1350. This time however, it was the costs that were talked up to '£1,600 in round numbers'. Too round. Costs did not reach £1,598 until December 1862. In August 1860, they were still £1,483. Hence, the paper's calculated shortfall of £250 compared with the real figure of £132. More subscriptions were requested in firm fashion by the editor. For good measure, he also solicited from the readership the formation of a proper library society to make use of the M.P.'s donation of £50 towards the purchase of books.

In September 1860, Holloway was again asked to produce plans, this time for outbuildings. The resolution, later in the month, was that the scheme for a retiring room and lobby be approved and put in hand forthwith. Pressure for expansion continued. In February 1867, the Corporation were already thinking about enlarging the hall and altering the retiring room, which had by then been built. It is the rear extension shown to the main hall on the 1870 map. They were also considering an infirmary development. A tender of £192 was accepted in May for certain alterations to the hall. Matters were being conducted with perhaps more confidence – the town had come a long way since the hesitations of the conversion versus rebuilding debate.

CHAPTER EIGHT

CONTROVERSIES AND COMMENT

Mostly connected with the relocation of the Third Town Hall, a considerable amount of comment and controversy over time was reported concerning use, management and even ownership. Yet at the same time, it is clear that the upgraded facility was immediately of great benefit to the town. The sense of humour, the level of irritation and in one case, the capacity for 'mild acrimony' of some townspeople, is all on display in 19th century Christchurch. It could even be that the 'True Humility' cartoon, by George du Maurier in Punch magazine 1895, is highly relevant, for instance concerning delays in starting the scheme and the disputed ownership issue, of which more, later:

> *Bishop: I'm afraid you've got a bad Egg, Mr. Jones!*
> *Curate: Oh no, my Lord, I assure you! Parts of it are excellent!*

However, at the end of the day, such disadvantages as these were too minor to count as 'bad' – in short, it never really was a Curate's Egg! Nor for that matter was there much evidence of True Humility amongst the participants!

A certain whimsical correspondent of the *Christchurch Times* habitually signed himself as Twyneham, the original name for the town which broadly translates as 'between the rivers'. Since the town has been known as Christchurch since the 12th century after the Legend of the Miraculous Beam, he clearly considered himself to be a sort of ancient guardian. He wrote as the personification of the town itself yet watching over it from his personal accommodation, deemed to be 'my Church Tower'. Although it covers other matters, this letter may be a classic of its type and is now reproduced in full.

> SIR, – Positively I think we are now stirring somewhat.
>
> I heartily congratulate myself and my people that we are "on the move." I remarked in my first letter that there was a great want of social intercourse among my people; that more intercommunication the one with the other, would abolish the self-exclusiveness which existed, and make them feel they had a common interest in joining together to make life sociable and happy. Since then, what have they

done? They are making arrangements to erect a new and commodious Town Hall, in a different and more convenient situation; which is to be, not as now a small room fit only for a few corporate and public purposes, but a real Hall for the use of *the Town.* Again, they are about to commence a reading-room in the present Hall, which is to be open from ten to ten, which is to be furnished with daily and other papers and some useful books, and in which my people from the highest to the lowest may mingle together for the common purpose of gaining instruction, and passing a social evening. What can be a better beginning than this? What can tend to unite more closely all classes than this? Upon my word I am beginning to be glad in myself: a *new* feeling is creeping over me, that of pride in my people; and I think there is really now a prospect of "good times coming boys." Let the promoters of the present movements go on in their good work, and I promise them they will reap a reward, by finding an improvement reflected in the intellectual and general state of my people, which, alas that I should have to say that there is so *very* much room for. It is a matter which if rightly carried out, will have an influence on the future prosperity of myself as a town, to an extent now little dreamt of.

Whilst thus engaged in seeking intellectual light, I watched my people carefully and anxiously, to ascertain how much longer they were going to put up with the so-called gas light furnished them by the gas proprietors. I was wondering whether my people being tired of life, were not really allowing themselves to be slowly poisoned by the execrable vapour nightly diffused throughout their shops and dwelling-houses; and all the while paying for the precious stuff at so much per foot. I was just giving them up when suddenly they roused themselves, and from being passive victims, became independent actors. They determined not to allow the gas to be forced upon them. They resolved to show that they were not dependent on the present gas works, and now they have begun to use other means of obtaining light. Let me tell them, they will disgrace me and themselves, if they treat with the present proprietors with a view to purchasing the works, until they are shown that the present works can make proper and pure gas, (which to me is doubtful); and until the proprietors have shown by their conduct that they are those with whom honourable men can deal.

I wish the little urchins who troll their iron hoops so constantly up and down my principal streets, could be told of the annoyance and danger they and their hoops occasion to passengers, especially those who are driving or riding. I have heard this practice complained of as a serious nuisance. Let them be told by those who have any influence over them, to play in less frequented parts of the town. If after a fair warning they are found thus annoying, I shall be obliged to tie one of them to my new pump as an example, and perhaps give him a thrashing.

Bye the bye, speaking of the new pump reminds me that I must congratulate my High Street people upon its erection; personally, or rather townly, I thank my Corporation for their attention to my wants.

May I venture upon one question, and I will then shut myself up in my Church Tower, silently and anxiously to watch over my people. That question is, – Where is my Burial Board? What have they done, or are they doing? Eight months have gone by since they were appointed. Have they in examining pieces of land for a cemetery, buried themselves by way of experiment, and cannot they come to life again?

Yours, &c.
TWYNEHAM

Christchurch, Nov 21, 1855.

We have here a master class in making political points in a humorous fashion, and no less effective for that!

Some months later, readers were treated to the views of Punchinello, a name from which Punch of Punch and Judy was derived. It most skilfully conjured up a surreal image and must have caused much amusement at the possible expense of the Committee. *Fig.16*, based on a painting from c.1830, shows an arched structure close to the middle of the road – it almost makes you think his suggested removal method was worthy of consideration!

PEACE DEMONSTRATION

SIR, – In all the municipal Boroughs, there has been a procession of the authorities, for the purpose of proclaiming Peace. We have not had such a procession, but I presume we shall have a demonstration in some way. Now I have heard a short time ago that the Committee, or some of the Committee, appointed to remove the Town Hall to a more eligible site, did really propose *actually* to remove our old Hall bodily, upon wheels or something of the sort, to a site they had fixed upon. Not having heard that the Committee have done *anything else*, I suppose they have matured their plans in this respect, and that therefore they must now be almost ready to try the experiment.

Would it not be a capital idea, and one for which I am sure they will thank me, to get everything ready for Her Majesty's Birthday, and to have a grand procession as a peace demonstration; in which procession our old Town Hall, in solemn march, might form a conspicuous and highly interesting feature. The other portion of the procession could be easily arranged so as to have great effect; for instance, the "oldest inhabitant" might be so placed as to have the overseer-ship of the whole and to see fair play. There are many other Gentlemen and antiquated Townsmen, who would prove great auxiliaries to the interesting scene, if properly placed; and *Twyneham* himself, if he could be induced bodily to appear, would prove not the least attractive of this exceeding attractive affair.

Now *don't* let this matter drop. I do believe it will so strike the minds of your readers with pleasing ideas, as to prevent their allowing the Committee to remain asleep.

There is one thing that I must urge upon the Committee, that is to be sure and issue notices and programmes of the procession as early as possible, because I am authoritatively informed that my relation *Punch*, is particularly anxious that one of his contributors and draughtsmen should be present on the ever-to-be-remembered, if ever-to-take-place-occasion.

Yours, &c.
PUNCHINELLO

Christchurch, May 14, 1856.

No doubt the peace referred to was the end of the Crimean War and he was conscious that Queen Victoria had been born on 24th May 1819. Punchinello clearly felt that the ten days from the date of his letter to the Queen's Birthday were ample to arrange such an engineering feat. At this time, alternative sites were still under review.

In May 1857, the newspaper decided there was a need for some strengthening of the moral fibre: 'All those who have complained so much, and perhaps with cause, upon the slow progress being made with the removal of the public Hall, may have the opportunity of showing there shall be no slowness in *their* part of the business; but that names shall be rapidly subscribed, with amounts against each, in proportion to the anxiety they *expressed* for the benefit of the Town. We shall see. Seeing, we shall report.' Interestingly, it has not been possible to find that the Subscription List ever was published, although it may have been missed. Moreover, if the paper did make any donations, they must have been done on a personal basis, because there is no item for the *Christchurch Times* in the ledger.

By September 1857, canvassers for subscriptions were reportedly meeting with 'scarcely a refusal' and liberal promises had been made by 'our

Agricultural Friends'. The record shows that excluding the Corporation and Admiral Walcott's family, there were a total of 72 private donations between the start of subscriptions in September 1857 and the end in July 1861.

Meanwhile, as the months went by, there seemed to be little evidence of progress with the relocation project. It was time for another letter, this time somewhat sardonic and from a correspondent writing as Telescope. Although the members were sensibly proceeding with some care due to the lack of funds, the writer saw the delay as caused by incompetence! Again, the whole letter is reproduced:

> SIR, – *Rumours.* I hear whispered about that Government is intending to purchase Hengistbury Head, and to erect two batteries thereon with stations for officers and men. That the men of the Coast Guard service have orders to be ready for work at a moment's notice. Is this true do you know? If so what intruders are expected; for whose warm reception are these John Bull welcomers intended? Give us your opinion oh thou sapient one.
>
> I hear too that some arrangement has been made between our fishermen and those gentlemen who claim the fishing as their exclusive private right down to the sea, by which arrangement bait may be obtained by the men, and an end put to the disputes that have lately been going on, (somewhat expensively I should imagine) between the conflicting claimants. Is *this* rumour true? If so it would be interesting to know the nature of that arrangement which has created peace.
>
> It was rumoured some long time ago that a New Town Hall was about to be built at Christchurch; it is *still* rumoured that there is some *intention* on the part of the Corporation, or on the part of somebody or other, to erect one. You no doubt know personally the members of that respectable ancient Corporation, but those who have not that pleasure (of whom I am one) can find no *acting* or *doing* by that body to evidence its existence; for my own part, I cannot for the life of me spy out a single thing to show that the Corporation are of the slightest use. However if the inhabitants of the town itself like to sleep on, while their neighbours are getting ahead, I have no right to complain. I know this that Christchurch is famous for talking, – nothing but rumour, rumour, rumour, – rumour of a Railway; rumour of a Town Hall; rumour of improvement generally; but where is the *acting*? "Actions, not words," is the motto for these days.
>
> Yours, &c.
TELESCOPE

Mudeford, May 6, 1858.

Despite such nudging for action from the likes of Telescope and the fact that it was now over a year since the land had been purchased, it was to be another year before work began. It was all such a mixture. Whilst the scheme was delayed, some were vociferous in their condemnation. Yet it is hard to say that such complaints were overdone because the reasons for delay were not publicised. Even if the relocation task was not that efficient, probably the main explanation was a shortage of funds. However, that was not made clear locally, witness the September 1857 press report of the highly exaggerated figure of £1,000 already received. Many must have thought: 'They've got the money. What's the hold-up?'

The general theme of 'all talk and no action' by the powers-that-be in Christchurch was taken up by Alpha in the same month concerning the New Town Hall. 'The scheme has dragged its slow length along... Cannot the Committee or Corporation or *somebody* do *something* to show words and promises and resolutions are not just empty shadows?' Since the Council had apparently been working on the problem without result since 1842, Alpha had a point. Yet not according to the next writer who signed himself 'Q'. Q thought Alpha should show himself worthy of the first letter of the Alphabet, and together with another correspondent who wrote similarly (Progress) 'clap his shoulder to the wheel!' Still in December, Alpha confessed he was powerless, yet as for other young men of the town, he craved 'other amusement than strolling about the streets or listening to a maudlin song in the public-house.' In continuance of this whole lesson in human nature, Progress also responds to Q with a sardonic masterpiece of a letter including: 'The changes which have occurred during the *sixteen years* it has been *under consideration*, are certainly marvellous, and I am sure the Corporation must have toiled hard, very hard, and wearied both body and mind to "get this cart out of the mud"...'

Although Q regarded this sort of complaining dependency culture as quite wrong, he kept on with great good humour. Firstly, he expressed the hope that Progress did not assume that name without some cause, and also the regret that the desire for improvement amongst the young men had not appeared until after the Reading Room was 'broken up'. However, his main broadside was directed at Alpha, as the extract below demonstrates:

> Alpha has a scheme evidently – he knows what he would do, if he had the *"power of some of them."* Let him unbend his frowning brow, and tell us good humouredly, what he would do. Clenching his teeth and frowning, will not advance either him or his schemes – but trying fairly to promote them may, and at any rate can do no harm. Smile again, my boy, I say to him, and think what you can do. Get into a habit of working out your own

wants, and not waiting for others to do it for you. If this habit doesn't improve our town, 'twill improve you. It may conduce to your own prosperity, and when your laudable efforts have made you perhaps a wealthy Tradesman, you will "smile" at the time, when you were a funny little shopman, crying out for committees or somebodies to help you, and gnashing your teeth, because no Corporation had been chartered expressly for your amusement.

It is an old problem – should people seek remedy by direct action, or expect 'somebody else' to do it? On balance, one suspects that Q was writing a little 'tongue in cheek' knowing full well that the representations and efforts of Alpha would be unlikely to be effective.

As we have seen, work began in May 1859, but the next month triggered what became a tremendously detailed wrangle about ownership. The anonymous correspondent, 'Incredulous', claimed that since the building was paid for by subscriptions, the premises should belong to the town and be administered by trustees, rather than be in the sole ownership and control of the Corporation. The Town Clerk for the Corporation, which owned the old premises and had bought the new site, disagreed completely with that argument. However, the dispute only gained momentum much later when the failure of two gentlemen to pay their promised subscriptions (£10 each) was published in the paper. A matter which might have been passed over turned at once into a hornets' nest! A copy of the September 1865 minutes of the Town Hall Committee together with a rebuttal by Rev. Joseph Fletcher and Elias Lane appeared in the edition of 30th September 1865.

In essence, these subscribers (both major figures in the town) withheld their money as they had believed the new hall would be in public ownership by way of a trust, not owned and run purely by the Corporation. They correctly pointed out that the great majority of funds came from subscribers, not the Corporation. Furthermore, they objected to the fashion in which the accounts for the construction of the building itself had been mixed up with the later current account of its running costs and income. It was a fair point to make. The most acrimonious and lengthy newspaper correspondence ensued involving the Town Clerk James Druitt, Fletcher, Lane and others. One writer 'regretted the rancorous feelings on matters of religion and politics; feelings which are a dishonour to and poison in the breasts of those who nourish them.'

Once the new hall had been open for a few months, it inevitably generated complaints about disturbance, placed as it was on a formerly quiet site. A letter to the paper shows strong feelings in the matter:

SIR, – I do think that the Town Hall Committee ought to interfere to stop such constant annoyances as we are subject to in the vicinity of the new Hall. At the best we have the nuisance of a Farm Yard in close proximity, and occasional risks of having our beautiful Hall destroyed by fire thereby, and on windy days our Shrubbery inundated with particles of straw. At other times we have one penny gaff and then another, stunning, drumming and fiddling all common sense out of our bewildered brains. How can a meeting be held there on an evening while that uproarious Theatre is tolerated, close under the eaves. If such things must be patronised, send them to Portfield, or Mill Plain, or somewhere where the Public will not be annoyed; or at any rate let them not render useless, this, one of the noblest Institutions of the town.

I am, Sir,
Yours respectfully,
ETA

Christchurch, November 20, 1860

A penny gaff was a popular mid 19th century form of entertainment for what would then be called the lower classes. It was unsophisticated, noisy and usually with an entrance cost of one penny. The 'gaff' part of the name derives from cock-fighting. Clowning, dancing, singing and exciting stories could all feature at such events which were simply produced, needing merely a piano. However, they were noted for loose morals and greatly disliked by many for that reason. Whether the Christchurch version in the Town Hall reached the same extent of debauchery as happened in London is unlikely, despite this letter. It must be admitted though that these sorts of events are not of the type that the *Christchurch Times* would have wanted to report, whilst the letter does give a fair description of a penny gaff! On balance, it is probable that the letter is an overstatement bearing in mind that the receipts section of the ledger gives a maximum of five bookings for the new hall that could have been such events up to the letter date.

Returning to more general comment, after the many years of complaints about the old unsatisfactory hall, there had been further complaints about the delays in providing a new one. Moreover, there was some comment that hall charges were too high. On the other hand, there were cases of favourable comment about the new hall. For instance, a fund raising bazaar for the Priory Church in September 1860 was most successful with 'the Hall tastefully arranged and decorated for the occasion.' Once it had been built, as can be seen in the next chapter, a good time was evidently had by many at the various social functions. In addition, there was some success with the Reading Room enterprise and the moral benefits that it was felt to bring to the town.

In summary, although the relocation of the hall on to a better and larger site simply had to be done for the good of Christchurch, as ever in such things, it was dogged by some controversy along the way. In the end however, such a project has to be judged as a whole. Since there are disadvantages in any scheme, they cannot be used to stop all progress, nor should they. At certain points, town leaders no doubt felt that there was no pleasing some people!

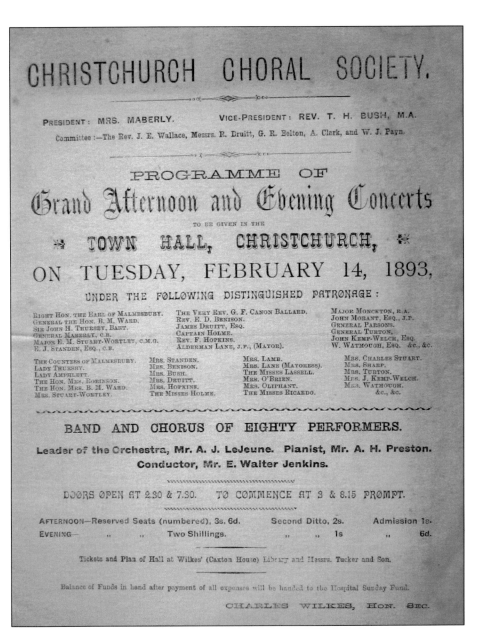

Fig.27

Christchurch Choral Society concert programme in 1893
(Reproduced by courtesy of Christchurch Local History Society)

Although an early complaint letter referred to the hall built in 1860 putting on 'penny gaffs', that could not be said in this case. Music included Merry Wives of Windsor by Nicolai, Voices of the Angels by Wilson, but mainly Barnett's Cantata of the Ancient Mariner.

CHAPTER NINE

TOWN HALL GATHERINGS

Some idea can be gained of Victorian Britain by looking at social functions in Christchurch. Many of these were held at the Town Hall and the reports of events (at both the old and the new halls) demonstrate just how much the rebuilding in 1860 improved things for the town. Yet without television or cinema, phones or cars, computers or modern appliances, effective health care or social benefits, the times were just about as different from now as they could be. In terms of lost aspects, it was a world of horses, firearms, workhouses and widespread poverty. It would certainly be more surprising if we did not find a completely different sort of entertainment from that common today. However, one sort, that continues much the same to the present time, is not featured below – the public house. Although beer drinking was widespread and necessary because water was far from safe to drink, it was not felt appropriate to encourage it at the Town Hall.

This chapter concentrates on the social contribution to the town made by the two Town Halls of the 19th century. The decision-makers in the town were of course the affluent, having senior positions within a very clear hierarchy. Corporation members tended to comprise such people, who generally seemed to be keen to uphold and enhance public morals. The same might be said to an even greater extent of the *Christchurch Times*, established in 1855. It follows that the halls were seen as a creative opportunity to promote the Victorian ethic, more than simply providing enjoyment for its own sake.

One particular form of entertainment that both the Corporation and the *Christchurch Times* were keen to encourage was the struggling Reading Room – struggling that is in both the old and the new halls. Such a facility was felt to be most beneficial to the town, no doubt as an early form of adult education and as an alternative to the public house. Both Holloway's plans for conversion and later, for rebuilding, included provision for one. As an indication of its perceived importance, even the Ordnance Survey map of 1870 (*Fig.24*) so annotates the front building of the Fourth Town Hall. However, it did need support from the inhabitants and effective funding for the reading material and hire of the room. Let us now look at some of the chequered history of the Christchurch Reading Room around the time of the Town Hall relocation.

On 3rd December 1856, a successful fund-raising Soirée, attended by 200 ticket holders, was held at the National School Rooms organised by the Reading Room Committee. The entertainment routine was a form of variety with earnest addresses interspersed with comic songs, glees and catches. A glee is an unaccompanied part song for three or more voices whilst a catch is a round in music, especially one in which the words are so arranged as to produce ludicrous effects. The review somewhat damned the skills of the performers, clearly identified for the benefit of the reader as amateurs: 'To make any particular remarks upon the vocal performances would be invidious...'

Before the National Anthem, Druitt spoke of the inconvenience of the room and asked the ladies present to assist the committee in raising funds for the new Town Hall – the 'hat would soon go round' he promised. In fact, the first private subscription was not received until 12th September 1857 – it was £5 in the name of White. The newspaper opined that one of the objects of the Committee was to 'break the ice and show that we Christchurch people *can* pass an evening in social intercourse.' It was remarked that in a novelty for Christchurch, different classes and sects mingled together most harmoniously, the only division being a partition across the room. Hence, encouragement to raise the funds for the room and new hall went hand in hand with the promotion of social harmony.

In the same month that the Corporation allocated purchase money for the site of the Fourth Town Hall, February 1857, another fund-raising social was held for the benefit of the Reading Room in the old hall. A most detailed report followed the second soirée. The Reading Room committee had considered at length, and in advance, the Great Tea Question, i.e. should tea be provided? Having decided against tea and indeed against any other form of drinks, the evening 'passed off very pleasantly', despite a forecast by some that it would be completely unattended. It provided entertainment for at least 100 people. The mindset of the times is so different from today that it can hardly be imagined. The Victorian principles, which wanted to see the new hall for the town funded by subscriptions, were the same principles used to promote donations and self-help to establish a thriving Reading Room.

The newspaper commentary perhaps requires some reading between the lines:

> We do not say that those who paid their eighteenpences for admission did not get their eighteen-penneth of amusement, laughter, and the pleasure derived from social intercourse, for we think they

most decidedly did; but we know the object of those who came forward as amateurs to join in a little vocal music, was not, moved by vanity, to presume to think their performances were entitled to the money, but, moved by a desire for a public benefit, to offer some inducement to parties, to give a little assistance to the library, which without such, might not have been obtained from them. The entertainment itself calls for no remark from us. Those who humoured the committee by attending, will be the best judges as to whether they did not do their best to entertain them." Mr. Bone addressed the assembly "assuring us that those engaged in agriculture like himself, were anxious to join with their town-brethren in any public good, and could enjoy as much as they an evening spent in harmony and social intercourse." The report concludes with satisfaction that "the funds have been materially increased, and that of itself is a satisfactory recompence to the committee.

In December 1857, the Reading Room Committee resolved to procure a Bagatelle Board and hold a musical soirée. Lectures, discussions and recitations were to follow, whilst the considerably improved Library was open every Wednesday. The newspaper continued to set the pace with an expression of surprise 'if all the young men of the town do not avail themselves of the opportunities thus offered...'

Just a year after the new Bagatelle Board, in December 1858, closure of the Reading Room was being planned. The paper deplored the cause – a want of subscriptions. It further deplored that few young men had enrolled. "This fact would appear to imply either that the providing a room merely for the purpose of reading two or three daily newspapers does not of itself prove sufficiently attractive for the young men of the town, or that such young men find other and less creditable employment for their evening hours." An editorial plea followed for funds to support the 'crying want' of a Mechanics Institute and the opportunity to mingle and know each other more. 'Is it not a fact that throughout the whole long winter, we seldom, nay *never*, meet together for any purpose save at our respective places of worship?'

In August 1860, the new building being fit for public use, the Corporation resolved for it to be freely available (when not required for a public object) to the use of 'any reading room, or scientific or literary Society'. The next month, any persons desirous of subscribing to the Reading Room and Library or of assisting in the formation of a Mechanics or Literary Institution were invited to contact Mr. Druitt or Mr. Sharp. Sadly, a year later, the Christchurch Reading Room was closed through lack of interest and to the predictable displeasure of the newspaper's editor: 'It is evident that the inhabitants of Christchurch and neighbourhood do not care to have a Public Reading Room and Library.' Part of the disappointment might have been that the November 1855 Reading Room project in the old building had been successful (at the start anyway) with 35 first class and 29 second class subscribers. The committee had even decided to 'admit Ladies, members of the families of first class subscribers, from 10 am to 6 pm.' Chess and draughts had been 'in much requisition'.

Once more the fortunes of the Reading Room rose above the problems. By 1865, it was operating very well as a library within the Working Man's Institute. At the half-yearly meeting in November attended by some 50 members, it was reported that there had been 700 books issued and re-issued over that time, around 30 per week. The balance sheet was healthy reflecting within the total credit and debit of £66. 9s. 7d., total book purchases of £16. 19s. 4d., and subscriptions of £26. 3s. Prospects of the Institute were described as 'of the most encouraging character.'

By 1869, the Town Hall was performing a main, if not leading, role in the town's cultural affairs. On one Monday in November, a special meeting of the Christchurch Working Man's Institute and the Society of Arts was held in the Reading Room. It was to consider a resolution that the educational board 'be earnestly requested to resume their labour.' It seemed that books had not been bought by the board despite the marvellous 27½% discount available as a result of the connection of the Institute with the Society. Yet if that benefit was no longer to be gained because the board were not buying books, then the Institute might as well make a break from the Society and save their subscription to the Society of two guineas a year. It transpired that the able secretary to the board had left the town and with the post vacant ever since, nothing had been done about buying discounted books. The resolution was duly carried. Perhaps the history of the Room shows a triumph of determination over apathy.

Moving on to more general types of entertainment, before the relocation, a concert was given by the Miss Hays on 30th September 1856 in the Third Town Hall. The reviewer remarked: 'Never was the want of a good public room felt more than on that evening.' The town's lack of a suitable venue had meant the loss of many potential lecturers and entertainers. The scene of this event was described as most provoking though ludicrous. The first thing was a rush through the doors when opened followed by the men struggling one with another to find seats for their ladies. Many were left outside as there was not enough room. Inside, 'stools and forms and chairs of all sorts were passed to and fro across the heads of the crowd.' Heat was intense and the space for the vocalists was soon taken up with tables taken down and the piano surrounded. Naturally, on the arrival of the singers, they could not see where they were supposed to perform, every inch of ground having been taken. But with great difficulty yet with good humour, they found an uncomfortable spot near the piano. The chief vocalist, Louisa, began with Annie Laurie, having Mr. Loder at the piano.

In the *Christchurch Times*, the wish was expressed for a larger room and a clearer atmosphere to do justice to her voice. Other songs followed to great acclaim: 'Wake me, early Mother dear', 'I 'spects I nebber was born', 'the nasty spiteful batchelor'. Much was achieved by the 'bewitching glance of her brilliant eye'. The youngest Miss Hay, said to be just five years old, sang two duets with her sister Alice, and Mr. Hay gave a description of Paddy Finn 'dining out with the jinteels', to the accompaniment of roars of laughter. In conclusion a laughing Italian trio was performed and the company sent laughing away. It may have been a success, but the hope for a suitable room for a future visit of these entertainers was fervently expressed. An estimate of numbers attending is not given, but working on Holloway's internal measurements of the first floor room, it was just 17 feet 3 inches by 43 feet 6 inches only, as punctuated by a staircase access – a squeeze indeed.

The first use of the room at the new hall was recorded in the ledger as on 8th May 1860 by a Mr. Greenhead and again the next day. The next recorded use was of the new hall, being a lecture by Mr. Harding on 15th May 1860 about the Great Social Evil. The paper described it as the 'monster evil of the day'. The Mayor expressed the wish that the heaviest penalty should fall upon the seducer in every case – as well he might from the tone of the report. 'Children who had promised in early life to become the sunshine of many a cottage home have filled it with a father's cursing and a mother's tears, and instead of being in their turn the pride of an honest worthy husband – their frugal table surrounded by happy children, the joy of their mature life, and the comfort and support of their old age – have lived only to be the mark of scorn and contempt, and died to have the short-lived memory of their names associated with ignominy to be as speedily as possible thrust into oblivion.' It is a prime example of the culture of the day being to take moral responsibility for social problems at a local level. Where better to press home such a message than in a brand new Town Hall to an estimated audience of 450 people?

Although it did not feature in the ledger of receipts, there is another story in the *Christchurch Times* of the very first use for the purpose of entertainment of 'our new, our noble Town Hall'. It was a programme by the Cremona Music Union on 7th May 1860, the report including the following:

> Music of a good order was successful in drawing a large house, as many as 380. Some attended probably from curiosity to see the interior of the new hall. A talented musical family of eight, in Cremona costume, entertained. It was styled "Our Bouquet" and was opened by some introductory observations by Lizzie. Other items included Rossini's Overture "Italiani in Algeria", "Buds and Blooms" and various instrumental solos.

In August 1860, the much bigger space was put to good use for a temperance lecture. It was to be a popular lecture from Mr. Ripley of the Christchurch Temperance Society. The subject was 'Common Sense for Common People', including a Melody (The Convert), a Recitation (Dream of the Revellers), a song (Oh Father! how we miss you) and a Recitation (The Maniac made by Rum).

The first meeting held in the new hall for religious purposes was on 14th September 1860. The Christchurch Auxiliary to the British and Foreign Bible Society found a full attendance on its twelfth anniversary meeting due to the accommodation being so much better than its normal venue, the National School Rooms. There were the usual prayers, a reading of the 67th Psalm and the Doxology was sung. The labours of the Society at home and abroad were reported, as were the numbers of Bibles and Testaments sold and moneys sent to the Parent Society. Gratitude was expressed for the Divine support and aid bestowed upon the agents of the Society. £10. 3s. 4d. was collected at the doors. All in all, it was a world away from the image conjured up by the strident complaint letter in the chapter on controversies.

On 18th September 1860, two most successful concerts were held in the Town Hall, the morning one for 'the *elite* of the town and neighbourhood'. The standard was apparently high despite the performances being amateur apart from the highly regarded and crowd-pulling Madame Sainton Dolby. One of the amateurs was indeed Sir George Pocock, the vendor of the Town Hall site. In the morning, pieces included Zampa, Mozart's 4th and 5th Symphonies, a Romberg symphony, a Rossini Overture and the Overture to Massaniello. The evening one was attended by some 300. Entertainment included the Three Fishers, the Skipper and His Boy, All Among the Barley and Haydn's No. 7 Symphony, amongst a number of others. It was a day of true musical appreciation at the new hall of a type that simply would not have been practical at the old one. There were many encores, much cheering and a sum raised of £73 for the Church.

In October 1861, there was a public meeting at the Town Hall of the Christchurch branch of the London City Mission. Four clergymen addressed the meeting explaining the sheer extent of the labours of the City Missionaries, e.g. '...389 Missionaries, who during the past year paid 1,815,332 visits to the inhabitants of those portions of the great city, which formerly were rarely if ever penetrated by any individual capable of benefiting that peculiar and generally miserable class.' The influence for good was considered to be incalculable.

In November 1869, the main hall was in use by the Working Man's Institute, this time for pure entertainment. The reader may agree that it would make a good night out, even today. Turns included: a Pianoforte Duett, Miss Tulloch and Mr. G. Ferrey, jun.; Reading T.P., a tale with a moral, Mr. Druitt; Christmas Madrigal, Choral Class; Recitation – Henry of Navarre, Mr.S. Newlyn; Song, Sweet Spirit hear my prayer, Miss Best; Glee, Jenny Gray, Choral Class; Reading, Paddy Flynn and Mr. E. Aldridge; Pianoforte Minuette and Finale; Madrigal, See our oars, Choral Class; Reading, The Frenchman and the rats, Mr. Pledge; Song, The Irish Emigrant, Mr. Bramble; Song, An Englishman am I, Mr. Burry; Duett, The Minute Gun at sea, Messrs Burry and Pledge; Song, Stonewall Jackson, Mr. Pledge; God save the Queen.

In February 1893, the Christchurch Choral Society gave two well-patronised Grand Afternoon and Evening Concerts in the Town Hall. *Fig.27* is a reproduction of just the first of a four page programme including an overture, songs, a glee, a rondo and Barnett's Cantata the Ancient Mariner. The Town Hall had truly arrived as a cultural force of some sophistication.

Fig.28

The Fourth Town Hall in 1860

(Reproduced by courtesy of the Red House Museum, Christchurch)

According to local historian Allen White, this extremely old photograph, including a troop of volunteer soldiers and a band, was taken by J.D. Cox just after the Town Hall was moved.

CHAPTER TEN

FROM 1860 HALL TO 1960 DEMOLITION PLAN

It was indeed a distinguished century for the Fourth Town Hall of Christchurch. Due to the far-sighted work of James Druitt, the Mayor and the Burgesses, a solid foundation was laid for an enormous long-term improvement in local administration. The extent of the immediate improvement can be simply judged – the old site became part of the road and the new hall was very much bigger with a large plot of expansion land included. When the demolition threat loomed, the only part worthy of retaining was the front section based on the design from 1746, yet that was under threat in 1960 along with the remainder. But first let us look briefly at the extensions.

After the relocation of 1860, it was some time before further extensions were considered. The Ordnance Survey maps of 1870 and 1898 both showed the front 'two storey rebuild' of the Third Town Hall together with the large rear single storey extension and small ante room addition. Plans dated April 1902 represented the next phase – a large two storey back addition including technical instruction rooms, Town Hall ante room, scullery, surveyor's office, lavatories, art room, art master's room, class room and further ante room. In June 1904, a grant was made of £475 by the County Council to the Borough in respect of building costs on the basis that the county would have control of the premises once built. The agreement enabled woodwork instruction to be given to boys and cookery and laundry instruction to girls. How times have changed!

In April 1923, a new ladies convenience was shown as a small north-west addition to the front section. In December 1923, the Council let the whole of the newly-acquired back land to the Boy Scouts for seven years at a rent of £10 per annum, an occupation that was continued thereafter as an annual tenancy. They were allowed to make full use of the ten-foot wide access way at the side of the Town Hall for horses, other animals and carts, laden or unladen. The scouts were allowed to erect a temporary hut but had to make the land available for the drills of the Christchurch Fire Brigade. Drawings, dated June 1933, reflected a further enlargement that increased the office space (at the expense of the educational function) added more toilets, a strong room and a new Council Chamber. In September 1943, a contract was let for the building of sleeping quarters, watch room and store as additions to an existing Rescue Depot. By December 1946, a large improved ladies convenience was designed to replace the 1923 one.

    As something of an aside, a recent minor mystery concerned an electrical junction box marked Gunfire Time Switch and served by a thick electrical cable from below ground level. It is fixed just below first floor level close to the blue heritage plaque of Christchurch Local History Society on the north-west wall of the 'Mayor's Parlour'. Although a little decrepit, it is still there at the time of writing (2009). It appears that Gunfire was a trade name for equipment made by the Automatic Light Controlling Company Ltd., a Bournemouth based firm, which was active until the 1950s. The company originally made switches to turn gas lighting on and off automatically to avoid the need for this work to be carried out manually at unsocial hours. The products were advertised as suitable for the 'efficient control of public lighting'. It is understood from an ex-Councillor that the Town Hall (as it then was) gained the benefit of extra street lighting compared to the rest of the High Street in order to make it 'stand out' within the street scene. The time switch may have been installed for this purpose. Incidentally, the summary in this chapter is not intended to be complete and for those interested, further research could well be fruitful.

    Turning to the main subject of the chapter, the 1960 approved plan involving the demolition of the Town Hall was most remarkable. Even by the standards of the day, it was felt to be excessive and fortunately, objectors won the day. Had they not done so, Christchurch shops would be very different now and instead of the 'Mayor's Parlour', we would have merely a memory. In terms of civic aspirations, it was similar to the 1860 plan – the members wanted better facilities for the town. Otherwise, however there were differences. It was on a much larger scale with new shops and increased office space. Furthermore, the Council were able to fund it in 1960 without need to depend upon subscriptions. But unlike 1860, the members needed and failed to secure Ministry approval. One might say that where Victorian patronage worked, 20th century local government finance failed, but that would be too simplistic – with such totally different eras, comparison is difficult. If there is a message in the story, it is one of sheer good luck. Had the Boundary Commission not been in the background at the time, the scheme would almost certainly have gone ahead.

    An early step was the appointment of Chartered Architects in January 1960 because 'the Corporation is proposing to erect a Town Hall and offices.' A Compulsory Purchase Order (CPO) dated 1st March 1960 was actually signed by the Mayor John Richardson and his Town Clerk. It was known as the 'Borough of Christchurch (Town Hall Site) Compulsory Purchase Order 1960' and enabled the acquisition of three rear land parcels of 0.71 acres, 0.15 acres and 0.43 acres. Added to the land already owned by the Council, these parcels provided a big enough site for comprehensive treatment. Throughout the controversy, Richardson was strongly in support of the plan.

The scheme showed a wide pedestrian entrance from the High Street with kiosks either side, instead of the Town Hall, which would have been removed. Behind this was to be an arcade with shops on both sides, each with rear service areas. Next, still going away from the High Street, a new road was envisaged from the Bypass and at right-angles to it. That road was to access both the service areas and new Council Offices and car parking to its north-east. Broadly, the plan comprised new shops behind those existing and a Town Hall with offices alongside the Mill Stream.

A surprising feature of the whole story is that the Councillors seemed somewhat unaware of this advanced scheme even at a meeting in May 1960 – the layout plan had been attached to the CPO at least two months earlier. Councillor John Smith asked for temporary offices to be provided as soon as possible, saying that the town's municipal offices were 'antiquated and more crowded than Piccadilly Circus!' He was told that plans had been requested and sketches would be placed before the Council 'before long'. Another comment was that 'people at a modern factory would refuse to work under such conditions as existed at the Town Hall.' Councillor Toombs expressed himself as 'shy' of temporary accommodation, saying that it should be left 'right out of the picture'. Councillor Richardson, who had signed the CPO, felt that the motion, if passed, would be 'telling those outside that the Council was afraid of the Commission.'

Bearing in mind the work of the Boundary Commission, some opposed the motion to erect temporary offices, one regarding it as a sign of weakness and a 'lack of belief in our future'. In the end, the motion was lost with the members preferring to wait for permanent buildings to be approved. Whilst they did not want to waste money on temporary accommodation, they were on balance, comfortable with the idea of an expensive permanent scheme. This view was taken despite the great abortive cost to the public if Christchurch did not survive as a separate Borough. No doubt one opinion behind such a view was a large newly-built permanent Town Hall would assist the Borough to survive as an entity. Last but not least, the Town Clerk reportedly remarked that there 'were no grounds available for the erection of temporary accommodation.' If that was right, the motion itself was somewhat misconceived. In the event, although the CPO plan was eventually lost, those with faith in the future of the Borough were vindicated about that aspect.

In July 1960, plans were approved by the Council for a Town Hall costing £187,624 plus furnishings. The artist's or architect's impression is of a classic 1960s structure of concrete slabs, being a large-scale cross between the Police Station in Barrack Road and the 1960s building at the corner of Wick Lane and the High Street (*Fig.29*). A large hall for 500 and a small hall for 100 were included together with much larger office space. It was remarked that the need for extra offices had been identified in 1956 and that conditions had become 'primitive'. Despite an attempt by John Smith to have it deferred pending the outcome of the Boundary Commission work, the members generally liked the whole thing, described indeed as a Civic Centre. A new hall was said to be required regardless of the findings of the Commission. At least, the CPO scheme had finally been shown to the members.

Fig.29

Scheme for new Town Hall with 1960 Compulsory Purchase Order

The idea was to comprehensively redevelop the land behind the existing Council premises. The Fourth Town Hall was to be fully demolished together with all its extensions and mainly replaced by shops. A new access road from the Christchurch Bypass, parallel to the High Street and Mill Stream, was to serve the much larger new Council buildings in this sketch. Placed as they were, there would have been future expansion land for them on the other side of the Stream.

After Councillor Smith's involvement, another veteran objector surfaced, Mr. W.G. Palmer. Yet the very same day (5th August 1960) that the *Christchurch Times* reported the start of his well-orchestrated protest, a letter of praise appeared from a correspondent, W.A. Goodenough. Hence, just when Palmer planned a protest meeting with speakers from the Council and the public, Goodenough praised the scheme in glowing terms. Basil Druitt however was scathing. What was the readership to make of it all?

There is little doubt now that the town has had a lucky escape, but (if one dare say so) it is not good enough to condemn Mr. Goodenough from such a distance in time. Many people then were looking to what they saw as a bright positive future without our current attitudes to heritage issues. 1960s architecture was all the rage whilst buildings like the Town Hall seemed to be merit-free relics. Expressions of the era included: 'We do not want to live in a museum', and 'Out with the old and in with the new!'

Mr. Palmer, a 75 year-old Highcliffe ratepayer, certainly knew how to run the campaign. A prominent quote from him in the first report is: 'It would be absurd to launch out on such an expensive scheme with the possibility of administration being moved from the town.' He considered that this scheme and the (much cheaper) one for a swimming pool were bound to lead to substantial increases in the Borough Rate. In contrast, Goodenough found both proposals 'refreshing' and congratulated the Councillors accordingly. He thought they were far-sighted, would make Christchurch 'something to be proud of', and should be followed up by tennis courts on the marshes!

Druitt made a strong case the other way, starting with the comment that 'civic centres' have been condemned as a cause of congestion and were incompatible with the next era of town planning. He went on to describe the plan as 'a masterpiece of bogus modernity that is to be the new Town Hall.' However, his main criticism centred on the unnecessary destruction of the front part of the Town Hall (today's 'Mayor's Parlour'). Here was a building that 'not having a shop-front, would stand up to scrutiny at close quarters.' Currently, most would strongly endorse his comment: 'What its successor will be like can be all too readily guessed from what happened on the site of Square House.' The final paragraph of his cutting letter needs particular emphasis:

> Posterity has a nasty habit of judging peoples – and their Councils – by their architecture. Perhaps this Council is gambling on there being no posterity [note: a reference surely to the Cold War] or on its having equally bad taste. But we cannot be sure yet about the first, and the second, one hopes, is impossible.

A week later still in August 1960, the plans were further condemned by two letter writers. Mr. S. J. Watson pointed out that the Council had, till now, kept to necessities, and yet just when urged by the government to minimise capital spending, had approved two expensive luxuries: the Town Hall and swimming pool. He also thought the remark about Town Hall staff working under 'slum conditions' was a stupid one. Moreover, A. J. Wise had no time for a previous writer: 'If Mr. Goodenough's idea of Christchurch is an ultra-modern and rather ugly Town Hall in one of the most attractive and architecturally interesting High Streets in Hampshire, and tennis courts on a marsh famous in the South of England for its bird life, I feel sorry for him.' Punches were not being pulled!

In preparation for the protest meeting on 7th October 1960 at the Town Hall, some 2,000 hand-bills were distributed in advance. Palmer was to propose the motion urging a referendum before the Council proceed with the two schemes, as seconded by Watson. To encourage maximum attendance, he said: 'I don't think it will be a very peaceful meeting, but then I don't like things too placid.' That day saw illustrations of both schemes in the *Christchurch Times* together with a description again of the main issue as seen by the objectors – a waste of ratepayers' money. To avoid anyone missing, the point the leaflets stated: 'Ratepayers beware! £200,000 of your money is at stake.' One has to admire the organisational skills of the protesters.

Unsurprisingly, the protest meeting was well-attended, vocal and effective. Voting was 125 in favour of the referendum and two against in an effort to 'check this rake's progress of the Council'. The Town Hall was a 'grand old building' and demolition would be 'vandalism'. The Council had to be stopped from pursuing a 'local inflationary policy'. Once the Borough had been forced to merge with a neighbouring authority, the new Town Hall would be a 'white elephant'. For the other side, the claim was made that the design 'would blend in with the old town.' The impression of the scheme, provided by the image in *Fig.29*, answers that claim very well.

Five days after the protest meeting, Palmer was on his feet again objecting to the plans at the CPO inquiry. The Town Clerk admitted that it was conceivable but unlikely that the Borough would be affected by the Boundary Commission. He also advanced the dubious argument that the Council were anxious to go as far as possible with the shops and new road anyway. Probably the better view is that this was a scheme that should be done fully or not at all. It was said that the whole key was the site of the present Town Hall and that development could not be achieved without the Council's plan to establish a new Town Hall on the site which was proposed. If that had been correct, Saxon Square would have been impossible.

Objectors whose lands were going to be taken had their say. One objector's advisor commented that the new hall was 'rather a long spread-eagled thing' to the possible chagrin of the architect. Comment was made in favour of using up to several acres on the other side of the Mill Stream for parking instead. For the organised protest group, the case was made for authorities needing to exercise restraint on essential projects and cut out the luxury ones like this altogether. Palmer did not mince words either: 'It was an unnecessary extravagance... it would be a crime to go ahead with the scheme.' The Council side talked about improving the prosperity, administration and appearance of the town. The Inspector, W. F. George closed the inquiry and viewed the land – a decision from the Minister was to follow.

As if everything that had gone before was just a 'warm-up', the protesters now got on with the real work – a Borough-wide petition was organised. There were 30 area organisers and 74 helpers under the central control of R. W. Arnold. The request of the petition (as planned at the 7th October protest meeting) was for the Minister to withhold consent to the Town Hall building project pending the report of the Boundary Commission. A month later, it was to be handed to M.P. John Cordle for delivering to the Minister for Housing and Local Government. Everyone was invited to contact their nearest area organiser and to visit up to 40 houses. The tactics had changed somewhat as the process moved forward – the plea for a referendum having fallen on stony ground, the petition was created in order to ask the Minister to block the scheme.

We next move on to the matter of the skeleton! It is not clear the extent to which the 'skeleton situation' was generated by the controversy. However, on 4th November 1960, it was reported that the Town Clerk received a phone call from someone saying: 'So you don't believe in keeping skeletons in the cupboard?' Naturally, he enquired what the caller meant only to be told to look out of the window. Sure enough, Mr. Macfadyen could see the head of a complete human skeleton hanging from one of the flagpoles. It was the first he knew of the practical joker's antics during the night. The fire ladder at the rear of the offices had been used under cover of darkness. A conspiracy theorist might ask: 'Were there any skeletons still in the Council's cupboard at that stage?!'

Support for the petition was 85% generally, whilst 34 out of 39 traders in the High Street were also in favour. Organiser Arnold said the traders had been canvassed due to the declared support of the Chamber of Trade for the Council's scheme. He concluded that the Chamber's policy needed an early reappraisal. A Freeman of the Borough, E. J. Slinn pointed out that there was enough space for an extension to the existing hall to give all the space needed. Furthermore, he thought: 'It would be a pity to rob the High Street of what I think is a very pleasant appearance of the present Town Hall.' Matters were just not going the Council's way.

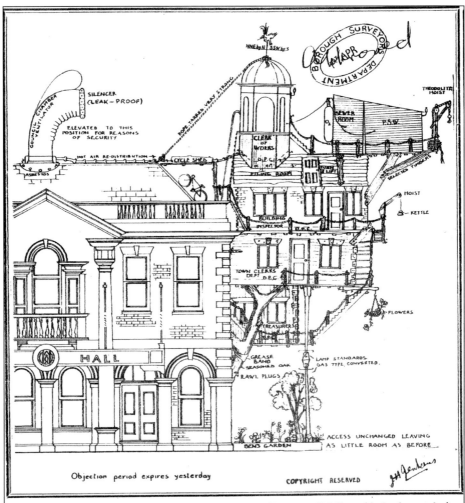

Another investigation by the Christchurch Council may well follow this further exclusive leak of a suggestion for extensions to the Town Hall designed to meet all the criticisms of Mr. Arnold, Mr. Watson, the Editor of the Christchurch Times and the remaining 7,564 persons who signed the petition against the Council's earlier plan.

This design—curiously bearing the mark "Approved"—was evolved by Mr. J. H. Jenkins of the Borough Engineer's department. We congratulate him on the originality of his ideas, on a certain fundamental logic in his design and his rather fine sense of balance. The whole thing is such a splendid breakaway from mock Gothic.

Fig. 30

Satirical sketch of alternative scheme from Borough Engineer in 1961

After the enormous protest about the sheer cost to ratepayers of the redevelopment plans and the desire to keep what is now the Grade 2 listed 'Mayor's Parlour', this more light-hearted contribution was made to the debate. From the grease band on the supporting oak tree to the perceived need for dealing with hot air from the Council Chamber, the sketch merits attention!

A week later, the skeleton mystery deepened – it had apparently 'done a bunk' after making a further brief appearance. It may have made a macabre journey to Christchurch from a Halloween party at Boscombe Hospital. The Council had locked it in a room at the Town Hall to await the reappearance of the miscreants. The paper thought they did so reappear, or alternatively, the skeleton broke out! One query posed was: 'Why, on Tuesday, was it being sought – in Highcliffe, of all places?' It seemed that Boscombe Hospital made no bones about it, saying they were 'plain angry at having lost the services of one of their skeleton staff'.

The headline on 18th November 1960 was: 7,567 SAY 'NO' TO NEW TOWN HALL. In a sense, the protesters had succeeded after all in their initial plan of holding a referendum – it was a 74% property return in respect of 210 roads canvassed. Whilst Arnold felt it was a clear warning to the Council that its scheme must be considerably revised, he still stressed the petition was not an attempt to block realistic improvements to the Town Hall. On 2nd December 1960, it was reported that the petition had been handed over personally to the Minister by M.P. John Cordle.

Fig.30 is a sketch from the Borough Engineer's department published in early January 1961. The stately well-proportioned elevation of the Town Hall is shown with what might be called a carbuncle on one side. However, a careful look will reveal an approval date stamp of 1st April, implying perhaps that this was not a serious alternative scheme after all!

Later in the month, the war still rumbled onwards. A motion, for ratepayers' associations to be invited to a committee meeting to listen to the reasons for the new Town Hall, was lost. Perhaps it would indeed have been a dialogue of the deaf. Yet it was resolved to ask the Minister to receive a delegation from the Council to have a general discussion about the need for additional offices. One councillor claimed that protest meetings were 'always attended by people against things'. In response, a protester suggested the Council should 'with good grace await the decision of the Minister.' The gloves were still off.

One of the main protesters had always been Councillor John Smith. He announced his resignation and walked out of the Council Chamber in January 1961, having failed to get the County Council's modifications to the town's development plan rejected in full. He was concerned about the character of the town being destroyed and the Town Hall being replaced. The attempt was described as another well-worn attempt to put a stop to the building of a new Town Hall. But as an Independent, he felt he could not continue to serve with members who were not (he alleged) carrying out the wishes of the electorate.

In March 1961, the Minister stopped the scheme in its tracks as 'premature'. In failing to approve the CPO, he clearly accepted the protesters' views about it being best to await the report from the Boundary Commission. The delighted instigator of the opposition, Mr. W. Gordon Palmer, duly congratulated the protesters in a public statement. Arnold applauded the brake which had been applied to 'runaway schemes for overspending local rate revenue'. However, it was felt that no animosity should be borne to those on the Council pushing the scheme – it was magnanimity in victory! But even so, a parting shot was fired by pointing out the real reason for the whole thing as perceived by the protesters: to present the Boundary Commission with Government approval of a scheme justifying Christchurch as a separate Borough into the future!

CHAPTER ELEVEN

THE 'MAYOR'S PARLOUR' TODAY

Before the final relocation of Christchurch Town Hall to Bridge Street, the Monday market was brought back. As from May 1976, after an absence of 105 years, the High Street was once more occupied by stalls on a regular basis. But there is one anomaly concerning present use – the lack of stall holders on the ground level of the 'Mayor's Parlour' as in times past. Apparently, the traders in the High Street tend to obscure the building so that, despite protection from the rain, pitches there are unpopular and licences not often requested.

By 1980, it was clear that comprehensive redevelopment would be desirable. The rear additions had 'grown like Topsy' over the years including some timber and prefabricated buildings. When the last move of Christchurch Town Hall was made to the new Civic Offices in Bridge Street in 1980, there was some salvaging of the temporary structures. A big difference from 1960 was the much better design quality of the new premises. It means that we have neither lost the best part of the Fourth Town Hall nor seen a replacement made from stain-prone concrete slabs.

There has been an enormous expansion in the duties and responsibilities of local government in the 120 years since the removal of the Third Town Hall along the High Street. The considerable rear extensions were demolished under 1981 consents in order to provide space for a new shopping complex. A key planning consent, for the Grade 2 listed structure, known locally as the 'Mayor's Parlour', was granted in June 1982 including alterations, refurbishment and rear wall rebuilding. This last involved reconstructing the wall of the rear elevation between the quoins. Existing quoins were to be made good in reconstructed stone. The stone balustrade and cornice were reconstructed. As the arches were being opened out, it allowed stone window sills to be salvaged from the High Street elevation and re-used on the Saxon Square elevation. The 18th century detached feel of the 1746 Third Town Hall was perhaps being recreated.

When the major commercial redevelopment of Saxon Square opened officially on 28th September 1983, it left the 'Mayor's Parlour' in the best setting it had ever enjoyed. Today, it is also used by the Borough for informal Council meetings and staff training. In addition, fund-raising, by local charities such as the Friends of Stanpit Marsh, is allowed on condition that an officer or Councillor is present. There is an annual event held for the Christchurch Local History Society. Up to 30 can attend without breaching any regulations. It can be hired for other purposes too, e.g. putting on a business breakfast, although it is quite expensive at a present charge of £30 per hour. Altogether, it is only opened up on average about once every week or fortnight.

It is difficult to place a value on the building now because it has both advantages and disadvantages. In its favour, here is a strong link with the past that is more attractive than most modern buildings and should be kept for that reason alone. On the other hand, there is a price for doing so, i.e. the limited use that can be made of it as an isolated outpost of the Council itself, allied to its significant maintenance costs. The roof has been re-slated, the gutters need regular clearing and roof leakage is not unknown. Pigeons do not help. The cupola suffered from rotted timbers some years ago and replacement left the structure less rigid. That was because those vertical supports that were fixed into the roof space had to be cut off and joined to new timbers with connectors. The consequent weakness meant that somewhat unsightly steel cross-bracing was needed within the tower, which had developed a tendency to turn. The cupola is a little strange in itself, being just a covering for a bell tower, which has not had a market bell in it since the 1860 relocation. On balance, it must be safe to say that the 1960 protesters were right to oppose the demolition scheme, planned exactly 100 years after the relocation.

It might be thought that a key aspect of the whole curious business is that for much of the time, we never appear to plan very well for the long haul and indeed, never did so in the past. It follows that buildings can sometimes be wrongly sited and need relatively early demolition. However, despite the restricted site of the Third Town Hall at that awkward road junction, it may not be fair comment to say that here. At least in this case, 113 years of use were extracted from it up to 1859 and since then, a great deal more.

The 'Mayor's Parlour' is now a most notable 'heritage feature' which visually complements Saxon Square. Its mere presence is a reminder of the strong feelings and debates about town matters in bygone times. Yet despite, or perhaps because of these, good decisions were possible – after all, following lengthy planning and weighing of the options in 1857, Blanchard's Yard was purchased to the great benefit of Christchurch. It must surely be fair to describe that judgement of Admiral Walcott, the Mayor, Burgesses and Inhabitants as extremely far-sighted.

INDEX

A
Alpha 70, 71
Arnold, R.W. 89, 91, 92

B
Bell, 17, 24, 25, 51, 53, 54, 94
Blanchard's Yard 13, 35, 49, 51, 57, 58, 94
Boundary Commission 84, 85, 86, 88, 89, 92

C
Compulsory Purchase Order (CPO) 84, 85, 86
Cordle, John 89, 91
Corporation Pew 32

D
Draper, Prior 15
Druitt, James 29, 32, 35, **48**, 57, 58, 71, 83
Druitt, Basil 86

E
Elliott, Edward S. 58
Equivalent reinstatement 55
ETA 72

F
Ferrey, Benjamin 22, 26
Ferrey, George 32
Ferrey, William 32
Fletcher, Joseph 71

G
George, W.F. 89
Gervis, Sir George 37, 46, 49
Ginn, Henry 5, 6, 8, 10
Goodenough, W.A. 86, 87
Great Social Evil 63, 79
Great Tea Question 76
Gubbins, George 57
Gunfire Time Switch 84

H
Hancock, Thomas 13, 14
Hastings, Henry 17, 18, 19
Hays, the Miss 78
Hengistbury Mining Company 32, 41, 47
Henry VIII 15
Hildesley, John 6, 17, 19
Holloway, George 32, 47
Holloway, John Edward 32, 39, 41, **47**
Holloway, Lewis v, 46

I
Inclosure Act 54
Inhabitants Committee 46, 49

J, K

L
Lane, Elias 71
Lavender, J.H. 53, 54

M
Macfadyen, Mr. 89
Malmesbury, Earl of 60
Market House 5, 15, 17, 35
Market Place 3, 5, 11, 12, 15

N
National School Rooms 59, 76, 80

O
Old Tolsey 1, 3, 4, 5, 6, 7, 8, 9, 10, 11

P
Palmer, W.G. 86, 87, 88, 89, 92
Penny gaff 72
Plague 19
Pocket Borough 19, 28
Pocock, Sir George 49, 58, 80
Punchinello 67, 68

Q
Q 70, 71
Quartley, Arthur 29, 36

R
Reading Room 46, 53, 63, 66, 70, 73, 75, 76, 77, 78
Rescue Depot 84
Richardson, J. 84, 85
Ripley, Mr. 80
Rose, Sir George 29, 32, 34

S
Scouts 83
Sharp, Mr. 58, 77
Skeleton 89, 91
Slinn, E.J. 89
Smith, John 85, 86, 91
Spicer, John 28
Strong Room 83
Surveyor of Ways 54

T
Tapps, George William 35, 36, 37, 39, 46, 50
Telescope 69, 70
Tolsey 1, 3, 4, 5, 9, 11, 12, 13, 15, 17, 21, 23, 53
Toombs, Councillor 85
Town Chest 51
Town Clock 37, 38, 39, 54
Town Goods x, 16, 17
Tucker, William 23, 28, 63
Twyneham 65, 67, 68

U

V
Vetch, Captain 34
Victoria, Queen 68

W
Walcott, Admiral John Edward v, 37, 39, 41, 44, 45, 46, 49, 57, 59, 94
Walcott, Charlotte 45, 59
Walcott, Constance 46
Watson, S.J. 87, 88
Welch, J.K. 61
Wells, James 54
White, Allen 9, 11, 18, 56, 82
Wickham, Mr. 60
Wylde, John 19